SEASONAL
Flower Embroidery

A Year of Stitching
Wild Blooms and Botanicals

Kazuko Aoki

ROOST BOOKS

Gente's Flowers

On a corner in the Tokyo neighborhood of Kichijoji sits the flower shop Gente. Step inside, and you will find the shop bursting with early-season flowers from the garden. A pleasantly intricate scent that combines *sweet*, *green*, and *earthy* envelops you. Familiar flowers are arranged with ones that you may have never seen to create the altogether different mood that permeates Gente's shop.

I invite you to enjoy with me these tidings from Gente for each of the four seasons.

How to make, p. 78 (Label)

Contents

Spring Gift

Outside there are still signs of winter, but the mimosa tree soaks up the spring sunshine. The mimosa's soft and fluffy flowers emerge from within small, hard buds—gather them up to enjoy their delicate and sweet fragrance, like morning dew. Miniature bulbs make a boisterous appearance, growing leisurely over the coming days. The way these bulbs naturalize and propagate is one of their charms. The gorgeous frills of pansies and their complex gradations of color create a timeless combination.

Spring's Canvas

We tend to think of spring colors as soft pastels, but pansies also come in chic and complicated shades—some are even the color of dark chocolate. Pansies make us realize that our sense of the season is displayed not only through a singular palette.

Another spring flower, anemones, are also known as windflowers. Their graceful petals are united by dark blue pistils and stamens. The more you look at them, the deeper blue they seem to be—and the purple variety appears even more mysterious.

Spring Tidings
from Gente I

#2

#3

#1 Soft, fluffy flowers that attract
spring's radiance

#2 Tiny, elfin bulbs

#3 A wearable brooch

Mimosa (#1), Muscari, tête-à-tête tulips, polychrome (#2), anemones (#3),
Yokohama selection pansies (#4), lily of the valley (#5)

#4 The complexity of these
flowers' hues is what brings
them together.

#5 The roots of this pretty flower
are quite hardy.

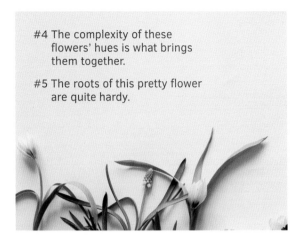

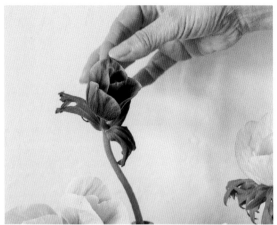

#4

#5

Mimosa Card & Mimosa Wreath

The adorably soft and fluffy flowers of the mimosa tree are recreated with so many French knots and spiderweb rose stitches. A chenille yarn from the Kyoto yarn shop, Art Fiber Endo, makes the French knots puffy enough on their own. The density and volume of the flowers on the mimosa wreath are very pleasing.

How to make, pp. 68–69

Muscari latifolium

Miniature Bulbs

One of the most charming things about these bulbs is their roots. Use stiff thread that will convey and highlight this detail. I used packaging thread here. I'm always on the lookout for materials. Stock up on any thread you come across that interests you.

How to make, pp. 70–71

Tête-à-Tête Pouch

This miniature tulip, tête-à-tête, is one of the original stock seeds. The red zipper fastener matches the color of the tulip's petals.

How to make, p. 72

Pansy Brooches

The more you look at the Yokohama Selection pansy, the more intricate its colors seem. Though these color combinations are challenging, there is something soothing about seeing them together. The frills on the petals are shown with clear, sharp lines of color. The other pansies I chose are called "Mr. Dandy" and "Fairy Princess."

How to make, p. 73

Anemone Brooches

The model for the blue anemone is called "Mona Lisa." The other two are based on "Porto," which is an Italian variety. The breeders must have used noble stock. Even flowers can possess aristocratic elegance.

How to make, p. 74

#6

#7

Spring Tidings
from Gente II

#6 A posy of forget-me-nots
#7 Spring bouquet
#8 Gathering white flowers
#9 A cake of violets

Shepherd's purse, grape hyacinth, forget-me-not (#6); leucocoryne, lachenalia, sweet pea, cyanella, geissorhiza, alstroemeria, tulbaghia (#7); bladder campion, dwarf columbine, achillea, watsonia, "Darling Pea," love-in-a-mist (#8); various violets (#9)

#8

#9

15

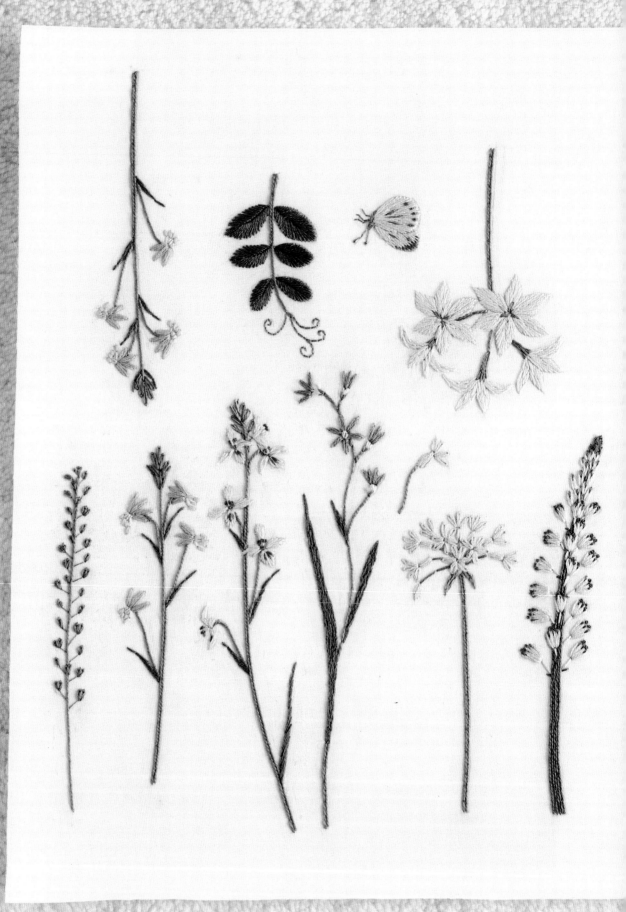

Spring Flowers

A small spring bouquet is delivered from Gente. I gently untie the bundle, revealing the fresh assortment of soft colors and various shapes and sizes of flowers, with plenty of sweet peas and greenery.

How to make, pp. 75–78

Spring Flower Cuttings

By cutting out and arranging flowers this way, you can create even smaller spring bouquets. They are lovely in any combination—you can make these extravagant flowers into badges or stickers or even use them as bookmarks. They're just like pressed flowers, aren't they?

Viola mandshurica

Argyreus hyperbius

Chair of Violets

If there were a chair made of grass, we could plant violets on it. Perhaps an Indian fritillary butterfly might flutter by and lay its eggs, then the larvae would eat the violets and turn into butterflies themselves. Because their diet consists of violets and pansies, they must recognize the flowers' scent.

How to make, pp. 80–81

Violet Brooch

Arrange violets of the same size as those for the chair of violets in a miniature wreath shape to create a brooch. My admiration of the antique violet brooch that Yoko Namiki, the owner of Gente, wears inspired this design.

How to make, p. 80

The Language of Flowers,
Lily of the Valley

For such a neat and clean flower, the lily of the valley is supported by
the hidden strength of its tangled roots. The sweet and refreshing scent
that wafts from its tiny pearl-like flowers signals the annual arrival of
spring and its attendant joy.

How to make, pp. 82–83

Lily of the Valley Basket Pouch

I made this pouch to fit inside a basket I found at Gente and decorated it with a small lily of the valley. The ladybug has a single dot made with a French knot. It is the slightest of stitches that manages to impart authenticity.

How to make, p. 82

Baskets

There's a trick to embroidering baskets. First, choose the two colors of thread that are closest to your favorite basket, then thread them together on your needle. Start by stitching the frame, then alternate the stitching just like you're weaving. It's the same process as weaving an actual basket.

How to make, p. 79

Gente's Baskets

The first time I received flowers from Gente, the arrangement arrived in a basket. The naturalness of flowers tucked inside conveyed a sense of the season and a pleasant spontaneity to the stems themselves. Hidden deep inside the basket was a container that held water, from which copious greenery sprung along with the garden flowers, and now the basket occupies a vital and familiar place in my life.

Gathering
White Flowers

Take time to gather the white flowers that bloom at the end of spring, heralding early summer. I set these against a bluish gray background, which calls to mind a scene in a Scandinavian forest.

How to make, pp. 84–85

White Flower Bag

When I set the same motif against a deep green, the colors appear completely different. To me, this is the fun to be found in the world of color. Once the bag is finished, you can take the grassy fields with you wherever you go.

How to make, pp. 84–85

Fritillaria uva-vulpis

Fritillaria persica

Fritillaria verticillata

Fritillaria meleagris

A Field Guide to Fritillaria

Fritillaries come in chic colors and have a carefree
appearance. I find the delicate coloring of the
pattern on the petals fascinating.

The Wellspring of Green

It's been many years since I first saw the work of Kazuko Aoki and its many expressions of lush greenery and grass. At the time, the flower industry favored distinct colors in flowers—smoky or ambiguous colors practically didn't even exist. And as for the greenery and foliage that play a supporting role in arrangements, I don't think there was much of anything beyond the "green" that resembles the crayon color.

When I went to Europe to study floral design, I saw with my own eyes just how many gradations of color exist—not only in flowers and greenery. I learned that those gradations themselves create a rich and abundant world that is itself art—but is also part of our everyday life. When I saw Kazuko's work, I identified with and was astonished by the diversity of gradations that she used.

I then reached out to a number of plant breeders and producers and asked them to create flowers and plants in all sorts of variations in color, shape, and fragrance. And now, many cultivars are available to be shipped to the Japanese market; some are even being imported from Europe.

I had always secretly hoped there would come a time when I'd be able to collaborate with Kazuko on some kind of project, and that opportunity has finally arrived. I take great pride and delight in Kazuko's love of flowers, her innovative designs, and in knowing that she is sharing the world of cut flowers with a wider audience.

—Yoko Namiki, Gente

Summer Gift

The beginning of summer brings a striking increase in the variety of flowers. Although roses can be found in the flower shops all year long, the summer display is all the more vivid. And it's also the time when berries ripen.

The petite flowers of the tea of heaven hydrangea are in bloom, as well as flowering branches and clematis. At this time of the season, you feel the connection between the flowers in the florist's shop and the flowers in the garden. It's a special season for roses too. Beginning with the heirloom varieties, all kinds of roses will soon be in full bloom.

Summer's Canvas

My visit to the secret rose garden also took place in early summer. Unbeknownst to anyone, the flowers bloom in the wild on carefree rose bushes and quietly scatter their petals in obscurity. Some roses dry on the bush, making them all the more beautiful. Finding a favorite rose among the countless varieties is a great source of pleasure.

Summer Tidings
from Gente I

Yoko gave me a tour of the rose farm, Ichikawa Rose Garden.
Inside the greenhouse chock-full of roses, the scent of roses is almost
overpowering. This is where Gente's original roses are created.

#1 As-yet-unnamed hybrid roses

#2 Ever so gradual nuances of color

#3 Testing out the fragrance

#4 Sowing seeds from ripened rose hips

#5 A charming green-eyed rose

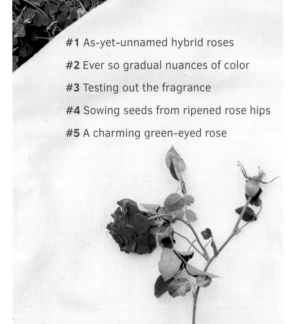

In the Rose Garden

Imagine a secret rose garden where roses that have yet to make their debut in the flower world bloom. The roses stretch their branches as they like and produce their blooms. A select few will someday be given names and will be found in flower shops.

How to make, pp. 86–88

Pink Roses

The phrase "in the pink" means to be in top form, excellent condition. Being enveloped by the fragrance of pink roses definitely makes one feel in fine form. By inserting a wire along the rose's stem, you can create your very own rose garden.

How to make, pp. 88–89

Rose Shears Case

Embellish this case for rose shears with your favorite rose. The rose shears from Gente come in a grown-up shade of rose pink. I chose to decorate the case with a single gorgeous bloom—and one bud.

How to make, p. 90

#6

Summer Tidings
from Gente II

#7

Juneberries, blueberries, raspberries, blackberries, and wild strawberries (#6); lavender, coriander, dill, apple mint, Italian parsley, German chamomile, and *Lotus hirsutus*, "Brimstone" (#7)

#6 Various tiny berries

#7 An herb-filled bouquet from Marufuku Herb Farm

#8 An abundance of fragrance from every flower

#9 Teatime in summer's shade

#8

#9

Chamomile

Chamomile from Marufuku Herb Farm

All the herbs that are used in these bouquets come from Marufuku Herb Farm in Kochi prefecture on the island of Shikoku. They give off a strong earthy scent, and you can sense how each vigorous herb has been nurtured on the farm. I traced a single stem of delicate yet hearty chamomile to embroider.

How to make, p. 91

Herb Wreath Bag

While carrying the heavy bouquet of herbs back to my workshop, I was inspired to sketch them and gently unbound their stems. The scent of the herbs permeated my small atelier; every time I opened the door, I inhaled deeply. These herbs had been cultivated without restraint, and as I sketched, they took shape as a wreath.

How to make, pp. 92–93

Berry Labels &
Berry Kiss Lock Purse

French knots and beads are perfect for representing the
tiny parts of berries. In this case, a minimal design makes
these small wonders all the more realistic. The labels can be
attached to pots of homemade jam as an ideal gift. One side of
the kiss lock purse is covered with berries; on the reverse side,
the polka dots look like scattered blueberries.

How to make, pp. 94–95 (Labels)
pp. 96–97 (Kiss Lock Purse)

Raspberry

Blackberry

Wild Strawberry

Blueberry

Juneberry

Autumn Gift

At Gente, I had the chance to take a flower lesson. We used autumn hydrangeas, wine-colored Queen Anne's lace, blackberries, and several scented varieties of herb Robert. With such subtly chic flowers, even those of us who were beginners couldn't help but create some of the most dignified arrangements I've ever seen.

The choice of flowers is so important. Start by selecting flowers that fascinate you, then decide on ones that complement your earlier choices. You might arrange them by color or put them together to highlight their contrast. This creative process is similar to choosing thread in embroidery—but in flower arranging, there is another important element: fragrance.

Autumn's Canvas

Herb Robert is an excellent companion for subtly scented flowers and greenery like hydrangea, Queen Anne's lace, and blackberries. Herb Robert's fragrance releases each time you touch it.

A beautiful bouquet that you have created according to the flowers' colors, shapes, and fragrances can sit atop a table and immediately call to mind the colors of autumn. Even as the color of the hydrangea fades, the petals will continue to bloom.

Autumn Tidings from Gente

Black ace peppers, rose hips, shell ginger, blackberry lilies (#1); Italian arum, black ace peppers, blackberry lilies (#2); autumn hydrangea (#3); cosmos, amaranth, *Lapeirousia*, burgundy Queen Anne's lace, Queen Anne's lace seed pods, ageratum, French marigolds, *Bessera elegans*, toad lilies, fountain grass, winter cosmos (#4)

#1 Chic shades of berries in a basket

#2 A wreath serves as a base for a mobile

#3 Thread in shades of green with autumn hydrangea

#4 A bouquet of autumn flowers

#4

Autumn Hydrangea Book Cover

The more time I spend gazing at autumn hydrangeas, the more incredible I find their colors. The green is tinged with blue and purple—creating hues that cannot be described with the names of colors we know. It's the perfect opportunity to combine strands of embroidery thread, letting us, perhaps, come close to the beauty of these autumn flowers.

How to make, p. 98

Autumn Brooches

Autumn ushers in a fleeting brilliance that is different from springtime's promise of lasting color. When the leaves on the trees start to change color, the cosmos are reaching the end of their prime, but the blossoms and leaves carried together on the wind create a seasonal mood.

How to make, p. 99

Autumn Bouquet

This bouquet looks as if it were gathered from a windblown autumn field, yet it carries such a rich and refined color combination. I sketched all of the flowers first in order to capture their loveliness. The novelty in this arrangement sets it apart from the typical flowers from the garden.

How to make, pp. 100–103

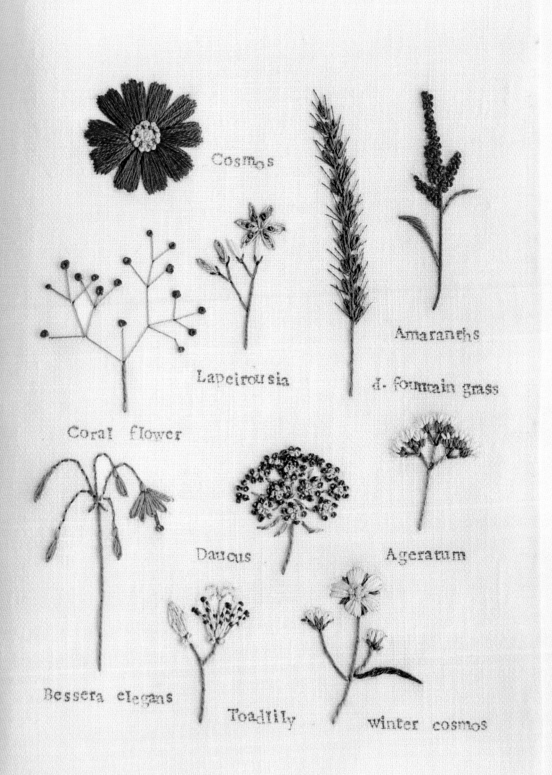

Cosmos

Lapeirousia

Amaranths

d. fountain grass

Coral flower

Darcus

Ageratum

Bessera elegans

Toadlily

winter cosmos

Winter Gift

Winter begins at Gente even before the end of autumn. If you're wondering what kind of flowers they have for Christmas, the answer is white and silvery green blooms. And when they use red, it's deep, rich red roses. The fragrance has to be that of an evergreen forest. And the indispensable shiny and lustrous winter berries at the end of the year bring hope for the next season. The flowers are greenish while the leaves are whitish.

Winter's Canvas

The flowers and leaves have been chosen for the delicate combinations they create. These quiet hues create a momentary respite for the eyes, overstimulated by the colors found everywhere else during this season.

The flowers used in a winter wreath have the texture and softness of flannel. They were chosen not for their seasonality but because their texture is so appropriate to this time of year.

Winter Tidings
from Gente

Flannel flower, *Phylica*, eucalyptus, dusty miller, globe amaranth (#1)

#1 Winter wreath

#2 Antique apothecary jar

#3 Evocative vases

#4 Flannel flower accents

Winter Panel & Dusty Miller Mini Bag

What I love about embroidery is deciding which thread to use and which stitches will create the desired texture, then thinking about the color combinations. For motifs as simple as these winter flowers, it helps to work some of the flowers in parts as you neaten up the entire project.

How to make, pp. 104 (Mini Bag) and 105–107 (Winter Panel)

Framed Flower Jugs

The vessel is important. A vase can change the entire appearance of a flower arrangement. I used to choose only simple, innocuous glass containers, so I was overwhelmed by the shelves at Gente, which are lined with vases, containers, and jugs selected for their textural interest. For me, choosing a few of these that I like is the first step toward progress.

How to make, pp. 108–109

Flower Vase Pin Cushions

First I made a pin cushion out of an iconic Virol jar. It has very small lettering, so I stitched along as I pictured what the wording looked like. I used a single color for the vase, which is shaped like an ornamental jar. It's not difficult if you go slowly, stitching one part at a time.

How to make, pp. 110–111

Point Lessons

Tools & Materials

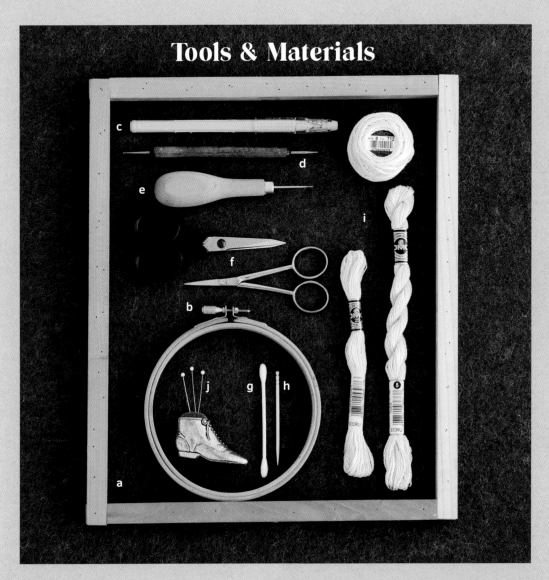

a / Rectangular Embroidery Frame
For larger projects, use a square or rectangular frame. Secure the fabric to the sides of the frame with thumbtacks.

b / Circular Embroidery Hoop
For smaller projects, use a circular hoop. Choose the size that corresponds to the project.

c / Chaco Pen
This chalk-filled pen is used for making light marks and for drawing patterns directly on the fabric. Lately I've been using a rub-off erasable ballpoint pen. The friction from the eraser or the heat from an iron removes the ink.

d / Tracer
This handy tool is used to trace patterns and transfer them to fabric.

e / Eyeleteer
This piercing tool is a savior for detail work. When I'm working with chenille yarn, I also use it to perforate the fabric before embroidering.

f / Scissors
I choose fine-tipped scissors for cutting thread, appliqués, fabric, and so on.

g / Cotton Swabs
Cotton swabs are indispensable for finishing work. Use a moistened swab to erase the pattern lines and to gently smooth stitches.

h / Toothpicks
Small wooden toothpicks are very helpful for applying quick-drying bond.

i / Embroidery Floss and Thread
I mainly use DMC embroidery thread, most often DMC No. 25 embroidery floss. I use DMC pearl cotton thread No. 5 or No. 8 for flower stems.

j / Marking Pins and Needles
I use marking pins to affix a pattern to fabric. I recommend silk pins because they are fine and the heads are small. For embroidery needles, what I use depends on the weight of the thread and what needles I have available.

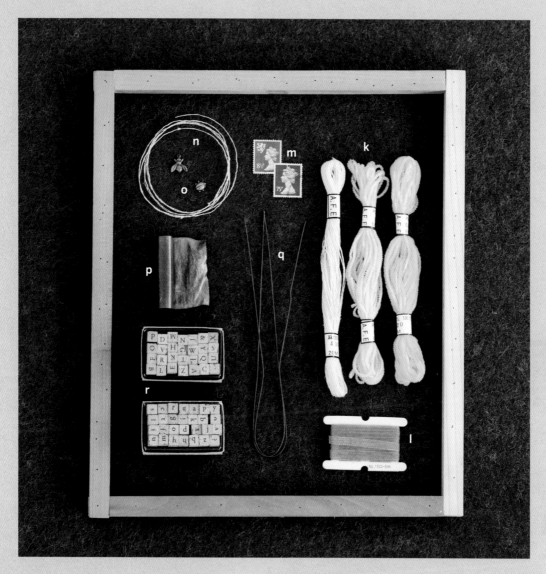

k / Additional Embroidery Thread
I also use Art Fiber Endo linen embroidery thread and chenille yarn.

l / Embroidery Ribbon
I use embroidery ribbon when thread isn't enough to create the effect I want.

m / Postage Stamps
I often use stamps like these as accents for projects. I recommend collecting some in colors you like.

n / Novelty Thread
This resilient cotton thread is used for wrapping. It's perfect for the roots of the bulbs.

o / Charms
Small charms add a little extra appeal to your projects.

p / Lead Sheet
I enjoy using this material for its interesting texture. It's very thin, so you can cut it with scissors.

q / Wire
One of my specialties is the variety of textures in the materials I employ. I use floral or annealed wire in various gauges.

r / Letter Stamps
I use letter stamps as accents. These inkpads are designed for use on fabric.

* In addition, of course, I use fabric as the basis for my designs and Chaco paper or tracing paper for transferring patterns onto fabric. Each project requires a different variety of materials.

Lessons on Finer Points

None of these embroidery stitches are difficult, but here are explanations for some of the finer techniques used in this book.

Making French Knots with Chenille Yarn / Mimosa Card, Mimosa Wreath

1 Because chenille yarn is thick, use a ribbon embroidery needle with a large eye. Before embroidering, use an eyeleteer to perforate the fabric you will be stitching.

2 Bring the thread through the hole, and wrap the thread around the needle. The size of the French knot depends on the number of times you wrap the thread around the needle. The more wraps you make, the larger the French knot will be.

3 Insert the needle back into the same stitch, pulling the thread tight with your left hand as you push the needle through to the reverse side.

4 Finished.

Ribbon Embroidery / Rose Garden

  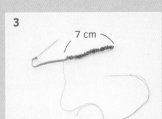 

1 Cut about 24" of ribbon, and thread it through the needle. Pierce one end of the ribbon and pull the needle through. This stitch secures the end of the ribbon to the needle so it won't come loose while you embroider.

2 Tie a waste knot at the end of the ribbon, and pull the ribbon through the fabric from the reverse side. Thread a second needle with a single strand of DMC No. 25 in the same color as the ribbon, and pull the floss through the fabric right next to where the ribbon comes out. Make a running stitch along 20" of the center of the ribbon. (It's okay if the running stitches are not even.)

3 Pull the thread on the running stitches, shortening the 20" center of the ribbon to about 3".

4 Coil the ribbon around in a circle, and pin it in place. Wrap a second coil, adjusting the gathers as you go. Pull the ribbon through to the reverse side to finish.

Layering Tulle and Other Fabrics / Chair of Violets

1 Layer the other fabric over the primary fabric, and use a sewing machine to stitch it in place. Using white acrylic paint mixed with a little beige, paint the fabric roughly, then allow it to dry.

2 When it's completely dry, remove it from the frame. Attach double-sided fusible interfacing to the reverse side of the appliqué fabric, then adhere it to the primary fabric using an iron.

3 Cut out the tulle, and layer it on top. Rather than using the exact same shape, I like to cut several similar shapes and layer them to add nuance.

4 To give the chair a three-dimensional effect, layer the tulle so that the back of the chair and the seat are lighter in color and the bottom part is darker and more shaded. Secure the tulle with marking pins, and machine stitch it in place.

How to Make the Brooches / Anemone Brooches

1 Embroider the flowers, then work blanket stitches around the edges. Sew the beads at the center one by one.

2 After embroidering, cut out the flower, being careful not to cut any of the stitches.

3 For the back fabric, cut out a shape just slightly larger, then glue it to the reverse of embroidery fabric. Trim any excess fabric.

4 Apply glue to the bottom flower, not just at the center but also around the petals that will stick out. Set the top flower, staggering the petals, and secure it in place. Press the center to make sure it's tightly attached.

How to Make

Notes on the Projects and Patterns

* Some of the patterns are actual size, and some have been reduced to 80% of their actual size. Where noted, please enlarge the reduced patterns by 125% for actual size.

* Stitch names are shortened in the embroidery patterns to their main name. For example, satin stitch will be referred to simply as "satin," straight stitch by "straight," lazy daisy stitch by "lazy daisy," and so on.

* The number in parentheses after the stitch name is the color code for DMC embroidery floss, unless noted otherwise.

* When DMC embroidery floss is not used, I recommend using Art Fiber Endo linen thread—though it is not widely available outside of Japan.

* In the embroidery patterns the type of DMC embroidery floss used is indicated by "#."

* When the thread type is not indicated, DMC No. 25 embroidery floss is used. Please combine and use the specified number of strands.

* For French knot stitches, the size depends on the number of wraps and the tension in the thread. In this book, use single wraps unless specified otherwise, but please adjust the size of the knots as necessary for balance.

* The fabric to be embroidered is specified in the materials lists as "Fabric," and other fabrics used as materials for the projects are listed under "Other."

* For fabric, the size specified in the materials list is the minimum amount needed, but since it can be difficult to work with small pieces of fabric, I recommend using larger pieces of fabric and trimming it down after embroidering your work.

* Most of the time, I apply single-sided midweight fusible interfacing to the reverse side of the fabric before embroidering.

Stitch Catalog

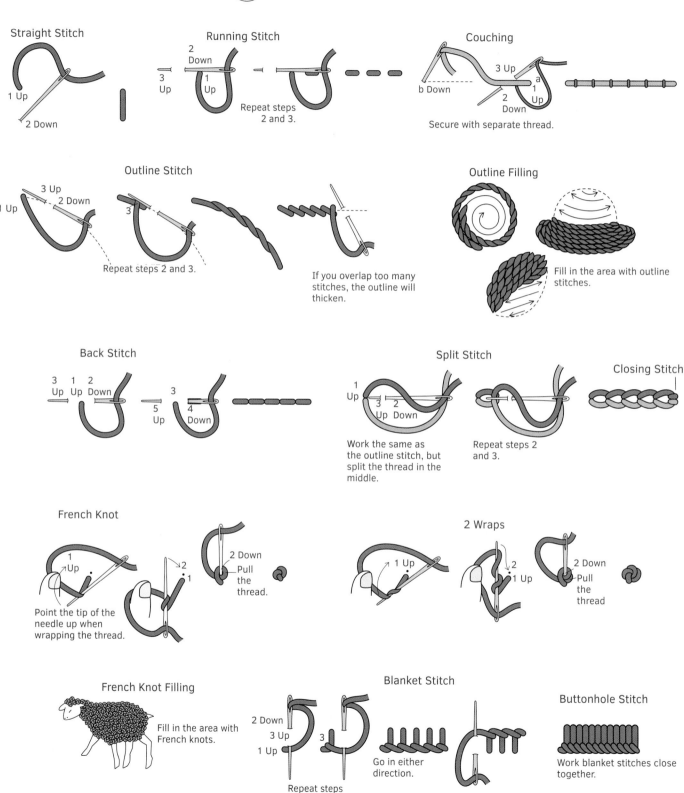

Straight Stitch

1 Up
2 Down

Running Stitch

2 Down
3 Up
1 Up
Repeat steps 2 and 3.

Couching

3 Up
b Down
a
2 Down
1 Up
Secure with separate thread.

Outline Stitch

3 Up
2 Down
1 Up
3
Repeat steps 2 and 3.
If you overlap too many stitches, the outline will thicken.

Outline Filling

Fill in the area with outline stitches.

Back Stitch

3 Up 1 Up 2 Down
5 Up 4 Down 3

Split Stitch

1 Up
3 Up 2 Down
Work the same as the outline stitch, but split the thread in the middle.
Repeat steps 2 and 3.

Closing Stitch

French Knot

1 Up
2 Down
2 Pull the thread.
1
Point the tip of the needle up when wrapping the thread.

2 Wraps

1 Up
2
1 Up
2 Down
Pull the thread

French Knot Filling

Fill in the area with French knots.

Blanket Stitch

2 Down
3 Up
1 Up
3
Repeat steps 2 and 3.
Go in either direction.

Buttonhole Stitch

Work blanket stitches close together.

Satin Stitch

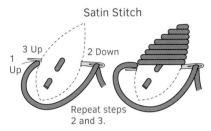

Repeat steps 2 and 3.

When the shape to fill in is large, it's best to start in the middle and stitch half at a time.

Padded/Raised Satin Stitch

First sew stitches underneath to add depth.

Long and Short Stitch

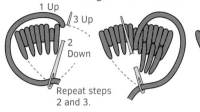

Repeat steps 2 and 3.

Work alternating long and short stitches.

Chain Stitch

3 Up   2 Down

1 Up

Repeat steps 2 and 3.

Lazy Daisy Stitch

Fly Stitch

1 Up   2 Down

3 Up

3

4 Down

Spiderweb Rose Stitch

Coil the thread, alternating over and under the radial stitches.

Weaving Stitch

4 2 6
Down

3   1   5
Up Up Up

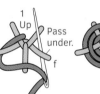

8 Down

Alternate over and under the vertical threads from left to right and back.

Bullion Knot Stitch

With needle still inserted, wrap thread around needle, and push wraps down with your finger.

3 Up

2 Down

1 Up

3

4 Down

Cross Stitch

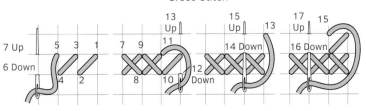

Mimosa Card

Thread: DMC embroidery floss No. 25 (12, 3347, 3364); Art Fiber Endo chenille embroidery thread (502, 520); Art Fiber Endo linen embroidery thread (417)

Fabric: Midweight cotton, white, 4" x 6"

Other: Fusible interfacing, 4" x 6"; quick-drying bond; card stock

Finished size: Refer to the diagram.

Notes: Apply fusible interfacing to the reverse side of the embroidery fabric before embroidering. Apply quick-drying bond around the edges of the embroidery; cut out when dry. Affix the embroidery to the card stock and tie with linen thread.

Embroidery Pattern (actual size)

Use 3 strands, unless noted otherwise.

After embroidering, use a toothpick to apply quick-drying bond around the edges of the work; cut out when dry.

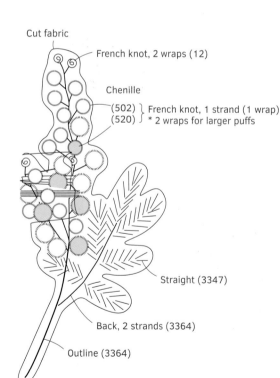

Cut fabric

French knot, 2 wraps (12)

Chenille

(502)
(520) } French knot, 1 strand (1 wrap)
* 2 wraps for larger puffs

Straight (3347)

Back, 2 strands (3364)

Outline (3364)

Mimosa Wreath

Thread: DMC embroidery floss No. 25 (12, 368, 822, 3346, 3347, 3364); Art Fiber Endo chenille embroidery thread (502, 520)

Fabric: Linen, white, 16" x 16"

Other: Fusible interfacing, 16" x 16"; cheesecloth, 8" x 3½"; text-print fabric, 1½" x 1½"; acrylic paint in white; cross-stitch canvas (14 stitches per inch), 4" x 8"; 2-mm-thick styrene board, 11¾" x 11¾"; bookbinding tape

Finished size: 11¾" x 11¾"

Notes: Apply fusible interfacing to the reverse side of the embroidery fabric before embroidering. Using the free-motion function on a sewing machine, machine stitch the cheesecloth and the text-print fabric onto the white linen, then lightly paint the entire piece with acrylic. Baste the canvas to the linen, work cross stitches, then remove the canvas. After embroidering the leaves, stems, and greenery, use chenille yarn to work the mimosa flowers (refer to page 64). Fold the fabric around the styrene board, then use bookbinding tape to secure it to the back.

Embroidery
Pattern (enlarge by 125%)

Use 3 strands, unless noted otherwise.

Using the free-motion function on a sewing machine, machine stitch the other fabrics onto the linen. Before embroidering, apply paint lightly to the embroidery area.

Use the canvas to work the cross stitches in the center. After stitching, remove the canvas.

After embroidering the leaves, stems, and greenery, use chenille yarn to work the mimosa flowers.

Pattern for center text   Cross, 2 strands (822)

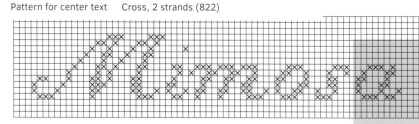

* Place the cross-stitch canvas in the center, then cross-stitch the letters.

Text-print fabric

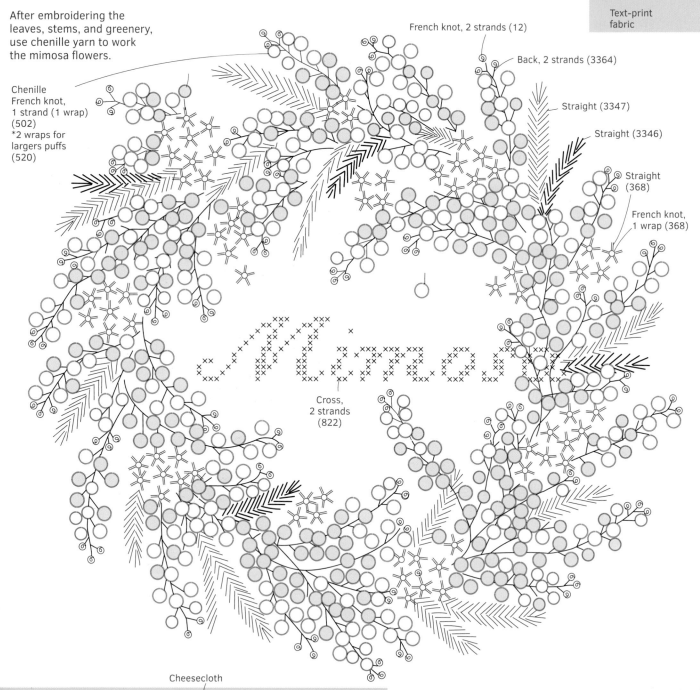

Chenille
French knot,
1 strand (1 wrap)
(502)
*2 wraps for
largers puffs
(520)

French knot, 2 strands (12)

Back, 2 strands (3364)

Straight (3347)

Straight (3346)

Straight (368)

French knot,
1 wrap (368)

Cross,
2 strands
(822)

Cheesecloth

Miniature Bulbs

Thread: DMC embroidery floss No. 25 (156, 157, 161, 368, 471, 632, 772, 988, 3346, 3350, 3363, 3790, 3835, 3862, 3866); DMC pearl cotton thread No. 5 (368, 471); different white thread

Fabric: Midweight cotton, white, 10" x 14"

Other: Fusible interfacing, 10" x 14"; quick-drying bond

Finished size: Refer to the diagram.

Notes: Apply fusible interfacing to the reverse side of the embroidery fabric before embroidering. Apply quick-drying bond around the edges of the embroidery; cut out when dry.

Embroidery Pattern (actual size)

Use 3 strands, unless noted otherwise.

Use No. 25, unless noted otherwise. "#5" denotes No. 5 pearl cotton thread.

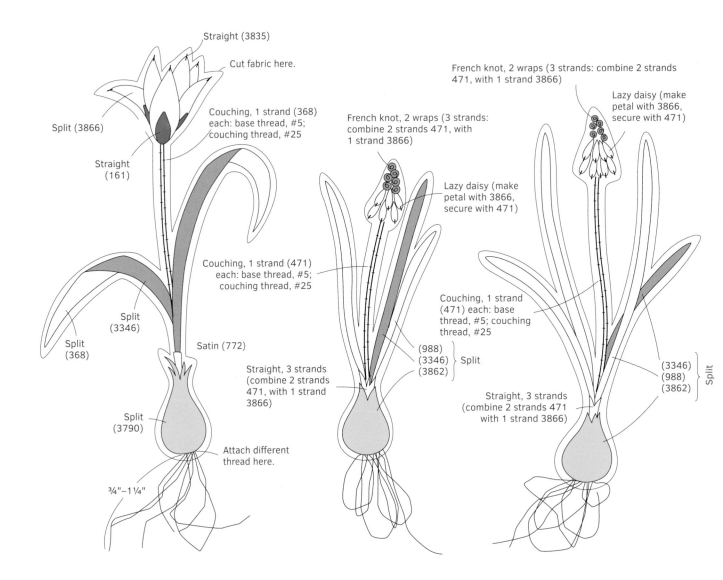

Straight (3835)

Cut fabric here.

Split (3866)

Couching, 1 strand (368) each: base thread, #5; couching thread, #25

Straight (161)

French knot, 2 wraps (3 strands: combine 2 strands 471, with 1 strand 3866)

French knot, 2 wraps (3 strands: combine 2 strands 471, with 1 strand 3866)

Lazy daisy (make petal with 3866, secure with 471)

Lazy daisy (make petal with 3866, secure with 471)

Couching, 1 strand (471) each: base thread, #5; couching thread, #25

Split (3346)

Split (368)

Satin (772)

Split (3790)

Straight, 3 strands (combine 2 strands 471, with 1 strand 3866)

Attach different thread here.

¾"–1¼"

Couching, 1 strand (471) each: base thread, #5; couching thread, #25

(988)
(3346) } Split
(3862)

Straight, 3 strands (combine 2 strands 471 with 1 strand 3866)

(3346)
(988) } Split
(3862)

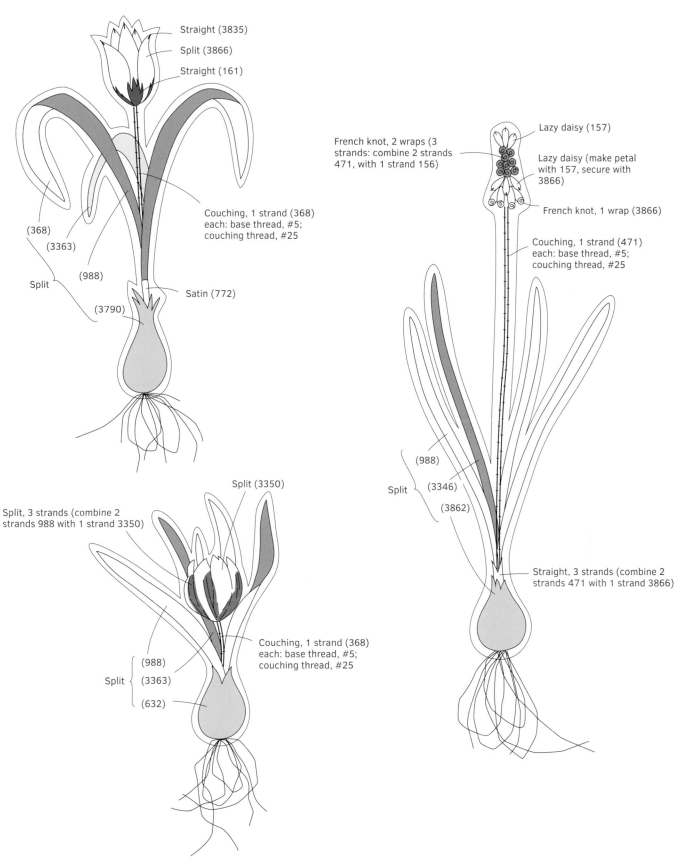

Straight (3835)

Split (3866)

Straight (161)

Couching, 1 strand (368)
each: base thread, #5;
couching thread, #25

(368)

(3363)

(988)

Split

Satin (772)

(3790)

French knot, 2 wraps (3
strands: combine 2 strands
471, with 1 strand 156)

Lazy daisy (157)

Lazy daisy (make petal
with 157, secure with
3866)

French knot, 1 wrap (3866)

Couching, 1 strand (471)
each: base thread, #5;
couching thread, #25

(988)

Split (3346)

(3862)

Straight, 3 strands (combine 2
strands 471 with 1 strand 3866)

Split (3350)

Split, 3 strands (combine 2
strands 988 with 1 strand 3350)

Couching, 1 strand (368)
each: base thread, #5;
couching thread, #25

(988)

Split (3363)

(632)

Tête-à-Tête Pouch

Thread: DMC embroidery floss No. 25 (347, 369, 779, 844, 937, 987, 3866); DMC pearl cotton thread No. 5 (369); Art Fiber Endo linen embroidery thread (401)

Fabric: Linen, sand beige, 8" x 12¼"

Other: Linen for lining, reddish brown, 8" x 12¼"; fusible interfacing, 8" x 12¼"; zipper, red, 6¼" long; grosgrain ribbon, reddish brown, ½" wide

Finished size: Refer to the diagram.

Notes: Apply fusible interfacing to the reverse side of the embroidery fabric before embroidering. Finish the pouch as shown in the diagram.

Finished edge

How to Cut the Pouch

- 7½"
- ¼"
- Opening — 1"
- 1½"
- Linen (outer pouch, lining), cut 1 each — 1"
- 12"
- 2"
- 11½"
- Direction of grain
- 1"
- Opening
- 4¾"
- 7"
- ¼"
- 7"
- ¼"
- ¼"

Embroidery Pattern (actual size)

Work split stitch, using 3 strands, unless noted otherwise.

Use No. 25, unless noted otherwise. "#5" denotes No. 5 pearl cotton thread.

Straight, 1 strand (844)

Tête-a-tête

French knot, 1 strand (844)

Couching, 1 strand (844)

(987)

(937)

(347)

Combine 2 strands (987) with 1 strand (347)

Couching, 1 strand (369) each: base thread, #5; couching thread, #25

(779)

Couching, 1 strand each: base thread (linen 401), couching thread (3866)

How to Assemble the Pouch

(1) Apply fusible interfacing to the reverse side of the outer fabric before embroidering.

(2) Place one side of the zipper at the opening between the wrong sides of the outer fabric and lining, and sew.

Fold the ends of the zipper.

¼" Opening

Zipper (wrong side)

¼"

Outer fabric (right side), front

Lining (wrong side), front

(3) Unzip the zipper, place the other side of the zipper at the other side of the opening between the wrong sides of the outer fabric and lining, and sew.

Zipper (wrong side)

Lining (right side), back

Outer fabric (wrong side), back

(4) With the zipper open, sew both sides together.

Lining (right side), front

¼"

Sew 4 layers together.

(5) Wrap seam allowances on both sides with grosgrain ribbon, and sew the ribbon in place.

Grosgrain ribbon

Lining (right side)

(6) Sew bottom gussets.

Lining (right side), front

1" 1"

¼" Side

Lay the side seam allowances toward back, then sew the 4 layers together.

Lining (right side) back

7"

4¾"

5" 2"

(8) Turn right side out.

Bottom gusset

(7) Wrap the seam allowances on the bottom gussets with grosgrain ribbon, and sew the ribbon in place.

Pansy Brooches

Thread: DMC embroidery floss No. 25 (33, 316, 327, 632, 742, 778, 3348, 3371, 3740, 3772, 3821, 3822, 3834, 3859, 3865)

Fabric: Lightweight cotton, white, 4" x 4"

Other: Lightweight fusible interfacing, 4" x 4"; felt, gray, 4" x 4"; quick-drying bond; brooch pin; sewing thread

Finished size: Refer to the diagram.

Notes: Apply fusible interfacing to the reverse side of the embroidery fabric before embroidering. Cut out the pattern, then cut a piece of felt in the same shape as the flower. Whipstitch the felt to the back, then sew on the brooch pin.

Embroidery Pattern
(actual size)

Use 3 strands, unless noted otherwise.

Work back stitches around the outer edges of the flower, then cut out the flower, leaving about ¼" of fabric.

Bronze

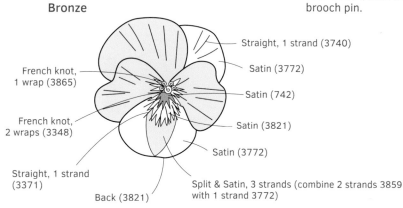

Straight, 1 strand (3740)

Satin (3772)

Satin (742)

Satin (3821)

Satin (3772)

French knot, 1 wrap (3865)

French knot, 2 wraps (3348)

Split & Satin, 3 strands (combine 2 strands 3859 with 1 strand 3772)

Straight, 1 strand (3371)

Back (3821)

Violet

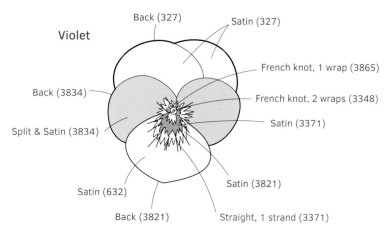

Back (327)

Satin (327)

French knot, 1 wrap (3865)

Back (3834)

French knot, 2 wraps (3348)

Split & Satin (3834)

Satin (3371)

Satin (3821)

Satin (632)

Back (3821)

Straight, 1 strand (3371)

How to Make the Brooch

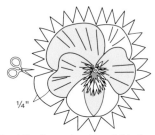

¼"

Cut out the flower, leaving a fold allowance of about ¼" around the pattern. Along the curves, make cuts in the extra fabric, then fold the extra fabric to the back and secure it with quick-drying bond.

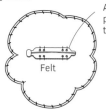

Felt

Attach the brooch pin slightly above the center.

Cut a piece of felt in the same shape as the flower, whipstitch it to the back, then sew on the brooch pin.

Pink

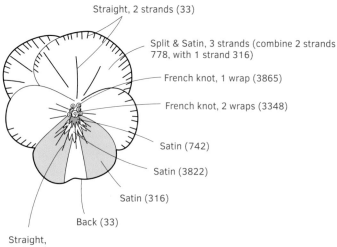

Straight, 2 strands (33)

Split & Satin, 3 strands (combine 2 strands 778, with 1 strand 316)

French knot, 1 wrap (3865)

French knot, 2 wraps (3348)

Satin (742)

Satin (3822)

Satin (316)

Back (33)

Straight, 1 strand (3371)

Anemone Brooches

Thread: DMC embroidery floss No. 25 (153, 823, 3746, 3807, 3866)

Fabric: Lightweight cotton, white, 8" x 8"

Other: Lightweight fusible interfacing, 8" x 8"; knit cloth, silver-coated, 8" x 8"; seed beads, black; brooch pin; quick-drying bond

Finished size: Refer to the diagram.

Notes: Apply fusible interfacing to the reverse side of the embroidery fabric before embroidering. Cut out the pattern, glue a piece of knit cloth in the same shape as the flower to the pattern, then cut around the edge. For the white and purple versions, stagger the two layers of petals as shown, and glue them in place. Attach the brooch pin to the reverse side (refer to page 64).

Embroidery Pattern
(actual size)

Use 3 strands, unless noted otherwise.

Work blanket stitches around the outer edges of the flower, then cut out the flower.

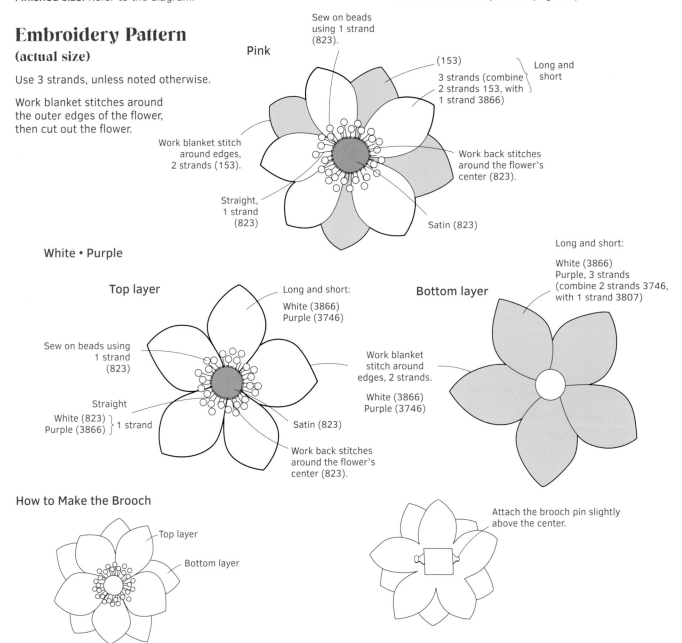

Pink

Sew on beads using 1 strand (823).

(153)
3 strands (combine 2 strands 153, with 1 strand 3866)
Long and short

Work blanket stitch around edges, 2 strands (153).

Work back stitches around the flower's center (823).

Straight, 1 strand (823)

Satin (823)

White • Purple

Top layer

Long and short:
White (3866)
Purple (3746)

Sew on beads using 1 strand (823)

Straight
White (823)
Purple (3866) } 1 strand

Satin (823)

Work back stitches around the flower's center (823).

Bottom layer

Long and short:
White (3866)
Purple, 3 strands (combine 2 strands 3746, with 1 strand 3807)

Work blanket stitch around edges, 2 strands.
White (3866)
Purple (3746)

How to Make the Brooch

Top layer
Bottom layer

Attach the brooch pin slightly above the center.

(1) Cut a piece of silver-coated knit cloth in the same shape as the flower, and attach it to the back with quick-drying bond.

(2) For the white and purple versions, stagger the 2 layers of petals as shown, and glue them in place at the center.

(3) Attach the brooch pin using quick-drying bond, then affix another small piece of silver-coated knit cloth on top of the pin.

Spring Flowers

Thread: DMC embroidery floss No. 25 (25, 153, 155, 157, 209, 211, 471, 612, 646, 754, 758, 760, 822, 840, 988, 989, 3347, 3363, 3803, 3819, 3821); DMC pearl cotton thread No. 5 (840, 989)

Fabric: Midweight cotton, white, 14" x 18"

Other: Midweight fusible interfacing, 14" x 18"; quick-drying bond

Finished size: Refer to the diagram.

Notes: Apply fusible interfacing to the reverse side of the embroidery fabric before embroidering. On the wrong side, apply quick-drying bond around the edges of the embroidery; cut out when dry.

Embroidery Pattern (actual size)

Use 3 strands, unless noted otherwise.

Use No. 25, unless noted otherwise. "#5" denotes No. 5 pearl cotton thread.

After embroidering, use a toothpick to apply quick-drying bond around the edges of the work, then cut once dry.

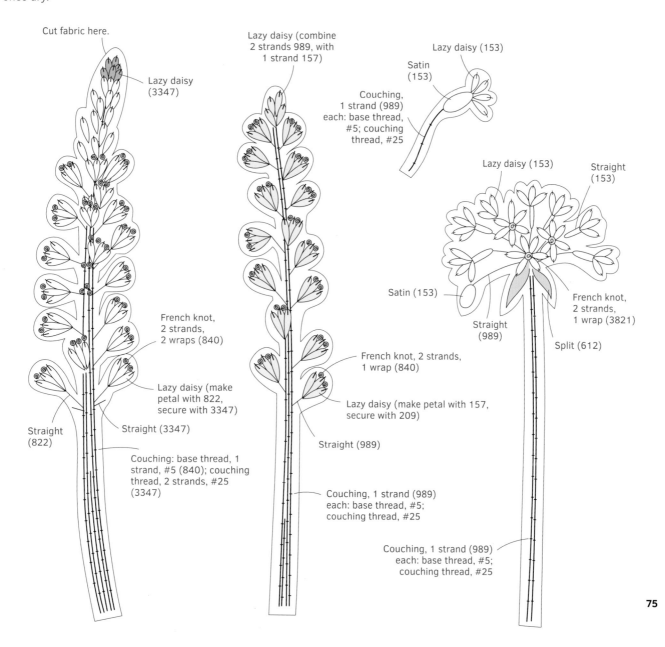

Cut fabric here.

Lazy daisy (3347)

French knot, 2 strands, 2 wraps (840)

Lazy daisy (make petal with 822, secure with 3347)

Straight (822)

Straight (3347)

Couching: base thread, 1 strand, #5 (840); couching thread, 2 strands, #25 (3347)

Lazy daisy (combine 2 strands 989, with 1 strand 157)

French knot, 2 strands, 1 wrap (840)

Lazy daisy (make petal with 157, secure with 209)

Straight (989)

Couching, 1 strand (989) each: base thread, #5; couching thread, #25

Couching, 1 strand (989) each: base thread, #5; couching thread, #25

Satin (153)

Lazy daisy (153)

Couching, 1 strand (989) each: base thread, #5; couching thread, #25

Lazy daisy (153)

Straight (153)

Satin (153)

Straight (989)

French knot, 2 strands, 1 wrap (3821)

Split (612)

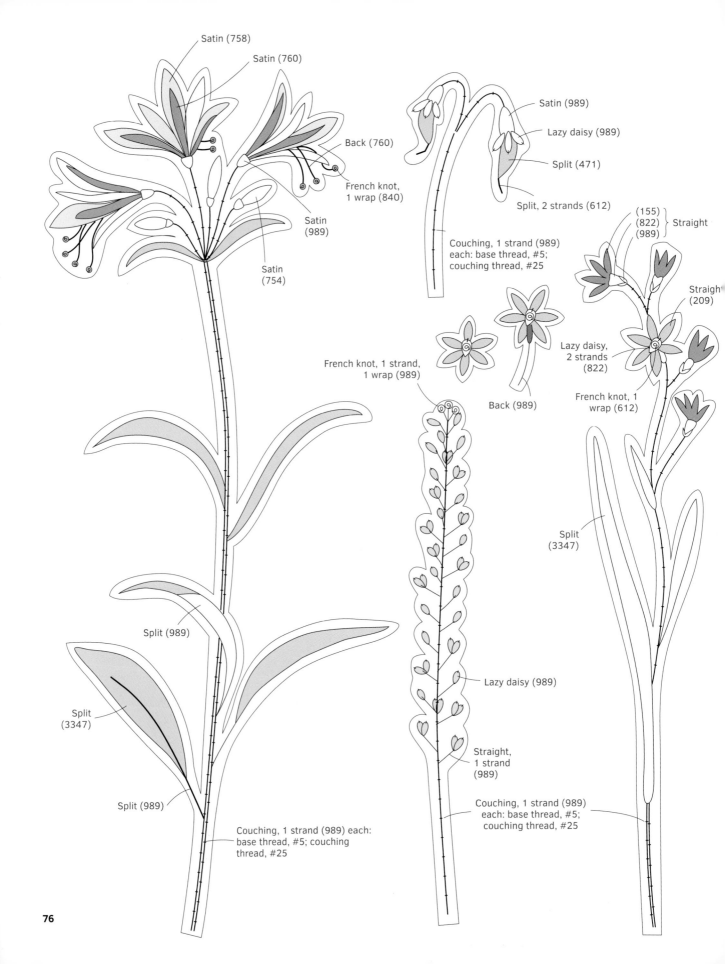

Satin (758)

Satin (760)

Back (760)

French knot,
1 wrap (840)

Satin
(989)

Satin
(754)

Split (989)

Split
(3347)

Split
(989)

Couching, 1 strand (989) each:
base thread, #5; couching
thread, #25

Satin (989)

Lazy daisy (989)

Split (471)

Split, 2 strands (612)

Couching, 1 strand (989)
each: base thread, #5;
couching thread, #25

(155)
(822) } Straight
(989)

Straight
(209)

Lazy daisy,
2 strands
(822)

French knot, 1
wrap (612)

French knot, 1 strand,
1 wrap (989)

Back (989)

Lazy daisy (989)

Straight,
1 strand
(989)

Couching, 1 strand (989)
each: base thread, #5;
couching thread, #25

Split
(3347)

76

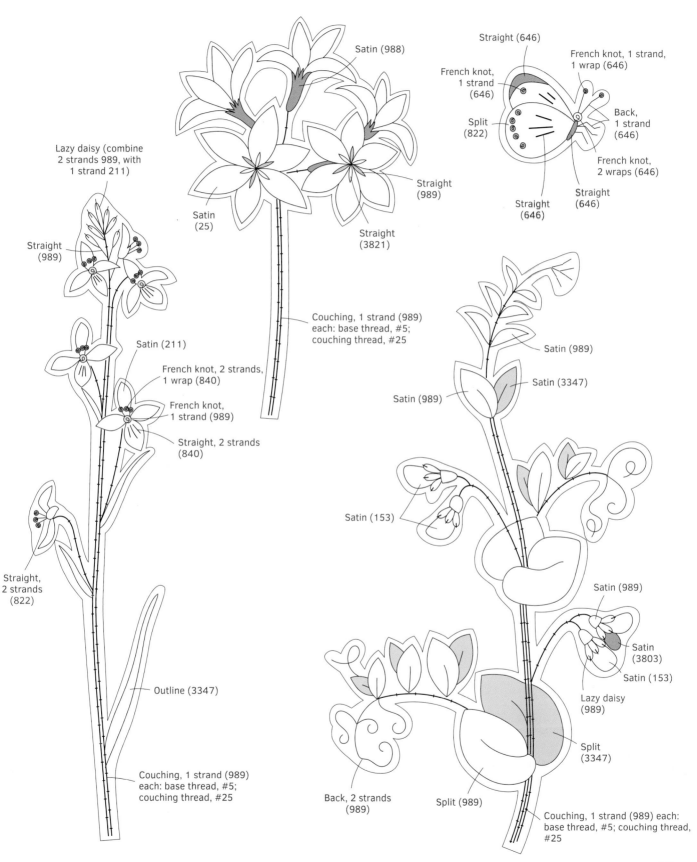

Satin (988)

Straight (646)

French knot,
1 strand
(646)

French knot, 1 strand,
1 wrap (646)

Split
(822)

Back,
1 strand
(646)

Lazy daisy (combine
2 strands 989, with
1 strand 211)

French knot,
2 wraps (646)

Straight
(989)

Satin
(25)

Straight
(3821)

Straight
(646)

Straight
(646)

Straight
(989)

Straight
(989)

Satin (989)

Satin (3347)

Satin (989)

Satin (211)

French knot, 2 strands,
1 wrap (840)

French knot,
1 strand (989)

Straight, 2 strands
(840)

Satin (153)

Couching, 1 strand (989)
each: base thread, #5;
couching thread, #25

Satin (989)

Satin
(3803)

Satin (153)

Lazy daisy
(989)

Straight,
2 strands
(822)

Outline (3347)

Split
(3347)

Couching, 1 strand (989)
each: base thread, #5;
couching thread, #25

Back, 2 strands
(989)

Split (989)

Couching, 1 strand (989) each:
base thread, #5; couching thread,
#25

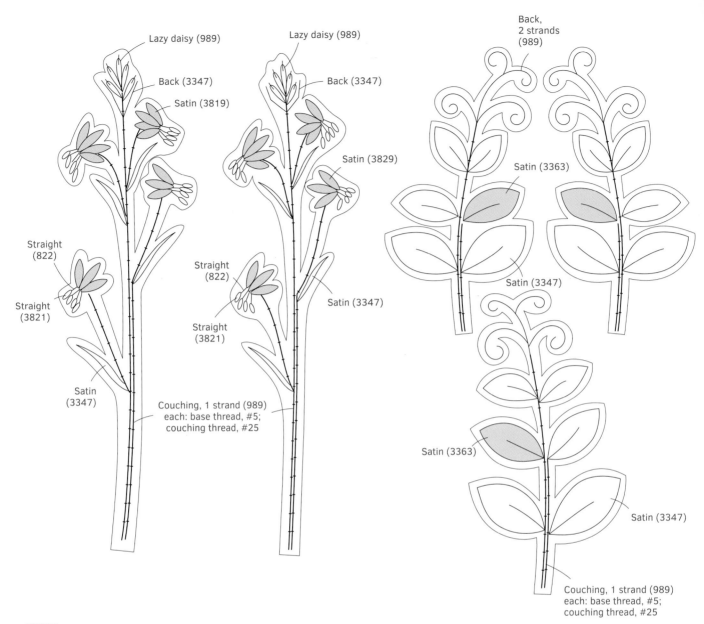

Lazy daisy (989)

Back (3347)

Satin (3819)

Straight (822)

Straight (3821)

Satin (3347)

Lazy daisy (989)

Back (3347)

Satin (3829)

Straight (822)

Straight (3821)

Satin (3347)

Couching, 1 strand (989) each: base thread, #5; couching thread, #25

Back, 2 strands (989)

Satin (3363)

Satin (3347)

Satin (3363)

Satin (3347)

Couching, 1 strand (989) each: base thread, #5; couching thread, #25

Label

Thread: DMC embroidery floss No. 25 (931, 3866)

Fabric: Cotton, white, 4" x 6"

Other: Fusible interfacing, 4" x 6"

Finished size: Refer to the diagram.

Notes: Apply fusible interfacing to the reverse side of the embroidery fabric before embroidering.

Embroidery Pattern (actual size)

Use 2 strands (931), unless noted otherwise.

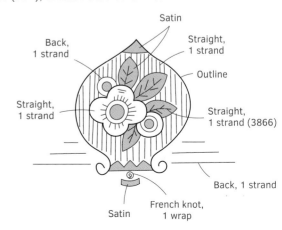

Satin

Back, 1 strand

Straight, 1 strand

Outline

Straight, 1 strand

Straight, 1 strand (3866)

Back, 1 strand

Satin

French knot, 1 wrap

Baskets

Thread: DMC embroidery floss No. 25 (435, 436, 3772, 3863)

Fabric: Midweight cotton, white, 10" x 12"

Other: Midweight fusible interfacing, 10" x 12"; quick-drying bond

Finished size: Refer to the diagram.

Notes: Apply fusible interfacing to the reverse side of the embroidery fabric before embroidering. Apply quick-drying bond around the edges of the embroidery; cut out when dry.

Embroidery Pattern (actual size)

After embroidering, use a toothpick to apply quick-drying bond around the edges of the work; cut out when dry.

Twisted Chain Stitch

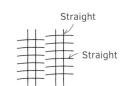

Make chain stitches, then build by entwining over each stitch.

Straight Stitch Filling

Straight

Straight

Make 2 lines of straight stitches vertically, then over those make straight stitches horizontally, 2 lines at a time. Make neighboring stitches so that the straight stitches alternate horizontally.

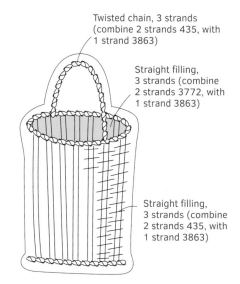

Twisted chain, 3 strands (combine 2 strands 435, with 1 strand 3863)

Straight filling, 3 strands (combine 2 strands 3772, with 1 strand 3863)

Straight filling, 3 strands (combine 2 strands 435, with 1 strand 3863)

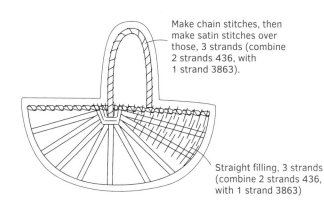

Make chain stitches, then make satin stitches over those, 3 strands (combine 2 strands 436, with 1 strand 3863).

Straight filling, 3 strands (combine 2 strands 436, with 1 strand 3863)

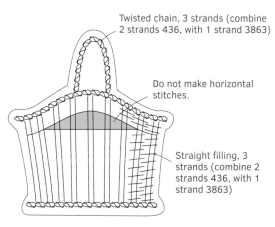

Twisted chain, 3 strands (combine 2 strands 436, with 1 strand 3863)

Do not make horizontal stitches.

Straight filling, 3 strands (combine 2 strands 436, with 1 strand 3863)

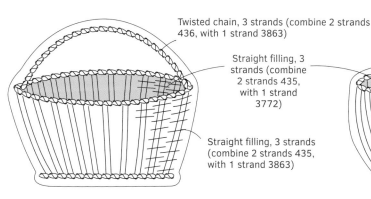

Twisted chain, 3 strands (combine 2 strands 436, with 1 strand 3863)

Straight filling, 3 strands (combine 2 strands 435, with 1 strand 3772)

Straight filling, 3 strands (combine 2 strands 435, with 1 strand 3863)

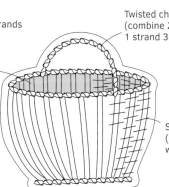

Twisted chain, 3 strands (combine 2 strands 436, with 1 strand 3863)

Straight filling, 3 strands (combine 2 strands 436, with 1 strand 3863)

Violet Brooch

Thread: DMC embroidery floss No. 25 (169, 729, 939, 3347, 3746, 3866)

Fabric: Cotton, white, 8" x 8"

Other: Fusible interfacing, 8" x 8"; linen, gray, 2" x 2"; floral wire, 22-gauge; 1½"-diameter donut-shaped showerhead brooch base; quick-drying bond

Finished size: Approximately 1½" diameter

Embroidery Pattern (actual size)

After embroidering, use a toothpick to apply quick-drying bond around the edges of the work; cut out when dry.

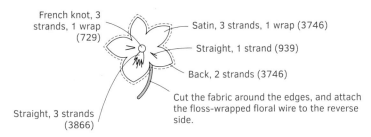

French knot, 3 strands, 1 wrap (729)

Satin, 3 strands, 1 wrap (3746)

Straight, 1 strand (939)

Back, 2 strands (3746)

Straight, 3 strands (3866)

Cut the fabric around the edges, and attach the floss-wrapped floral wire to the reverse side.

How to Make the Brooch

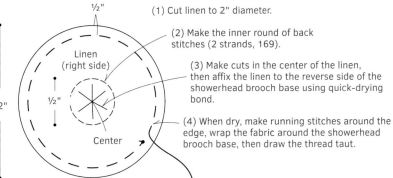

Linen (right side)

Center

½"

½"

2"

(1) Cut linen to 2" diameter.

(2) Make the inner round of back stitches (2 strands, 169).

(3) Make cuts in the center of the linen, then affix the linen to the reverse side of the showerhead brooch base using quick-drying bond.

(4) When dry, make running stitches around the edge, wrap the fabric around the showerhead brooch base, then draw the thread taut.

Notes: Apply fusible interfacing to the reverse side of the embroidery fabric before embroidering. Apply quick-drying bond around the edges of the embroidery, then cut when dry. Using floral wire, make the stem and attach it to the reverse side of the violets (make 5). Assemble the flowers on the linen as you work, attaching to the donut-shaped brooch base. Arrange the violets evenly and affix them with quick-drying bond.

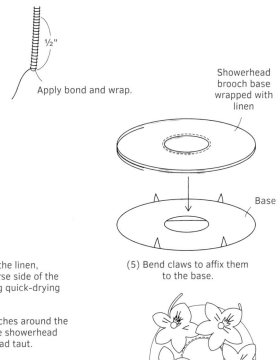

Apply quick-drying bond to the floral wire, then wrap it with embroidery floss (3 strands, 3347) cut to ½" length. Make 5.

½"

Apply bond and wrap.

Showerhead brooch base wrapped with linen

Base

(5) Bend claws to affix them to the base.

(6) Attach 5 violets using quick-drying bond.

Chair of Violets

Thread: DMC embroidery floss No. 25 (10, 12, 370, 645, 729, 782, 844, 907, 939, 3746, 3830, 3866); DMC pearl cotton thread No. 5 (989); Art Fiber Endo linen embroidery thread (213, 613)

Fabric: Linen, white, 16" x 16"

Other: Fusible interfacing, 16" x 16"; cotton, green, 8" x 8"; tulle, dark green, 8" x 8"; organdy, light green, 6" x 2"; double-sided fusible interfacing, 6" x 2"; cheesecloth, 8" x 4"; text-print fabric, 1¼" x 2¾"; lead sheet; acrylic paint, white; bookbinding tape; ½"-thick by 1½"-wide wooden frame; small nails or staples (24); letter stamps; inkpad for use on fabric (sepia)

Finished size: 9¾" x 10¾"

Notes: Apply fusible interfacing to the reverse side of the embroidery fabric. Cut the cotton and tulle into the shape of a chair. Layer these, then use the free-motion function on a sewing machine to machine stitch them together. Machine stitch the cheesecloth and text-print fabric together, then lightly paint the entire piece with acrylic. When dry, embroider the pattern. Cut 2 chair legs from the lead. Apply double-sided fusible interfacing to the organdy, then attach the chair legs using quick-drying bond. Stamp the lettering. Fold the fabric over the wooden frame, attaching it with staples or nails and securing it on the back with bookbinding tape.

Embroidery Pattern (enlarge by 125%)

Use 3 strands, unless noted otherwise.

Using the free-motion function on a sewing machine, machine stitch the other fabrics together. Paint the cheesecloth and text-print fabric with acrylic before embroidering, applying paint lightly to the embroidery area.

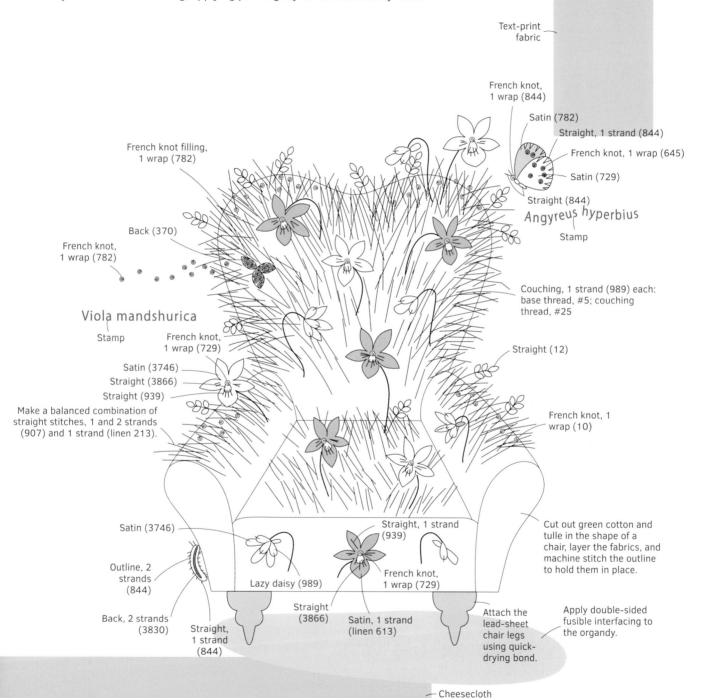

Text-print fabric

French knot, 1 wrap (844)

Satin (782)

Straight, 1 strand (844)

French knot, 1 wrap (645)

Satin (729)

Straight (844)

Angyreus hyperbius

Stamp

French knot filling, 1 wrap (782)

Back (370)

French knot, 1 wrap (782)

Couching, 1 strand (989) each: base thread, #5; couching thread, #25

Viola mandshurica

Stamp

French knot, 1 wrap (729)

Straight (12)

Satin (3746)
Straight (3866)
Straight (939)

Make a balanced combination of straight stitches, 1 and 2 strands (907) and 1 strand (linen 213).

French knot, 1 wrap (10)

Satin (3746)

Straight, 1 strand (939)

Cut out green cotton and tulle in the shape of a chair, layer the fabrics, and machine stitch the outline to hold them in place.

Outline, 2 strands (844)

Lazy daisy (989)

French knot, 1 wrap (729)

Apply double-sided fusible interfacing to the organdy.

Back, 2 strands (3830)

Straight, 1 strand (844)

Straight (3866)

Satin, 1 strand (linen 613)

Attach the lead-sheet chair legs using quick-drying bond.

Cheesecloth

Lily of the Valley Basket Pouch

Thread: DMC embroidery floss No. 25 (471, 931, 988, 3328, 3846, 3866)

Fabric: Linen, beige, 13¾" x 31½"

Other: Fusible interfacing, 9¾" x 4"; 5-mm waxed cotton cord, brown, 29½" long, two pieces

Finished size: Refer to the diagram.

Notes: Apply fusible interfacing to the reverse side of the fabric before embroidering. When making the pouch, pass the cord through the opening.

How to Cut the Pouch

- 11¾"
- Opening
- 1½"
- ¾"
- 11"
- 2¾"
- 3½"
- RETURN OF HAPPINESS
- Bottom of opening
- Bottom of opening
- Position of embroidery (only on one side)
- 12½"
- 11"
- Side (cut 2)
- Direction of grain
- 9½"
- ½"
- 10½"

- 6¾"
- Bottom (cut 1)
- 6"
- ½"

How to Make the Pouch

(1) Finish seam allowances with a zigzag machine stitch.
(2) Apply fusible interfacing to the reverse side of the fabric before embroidering. Trim excess fusible interfacing after embroidering.

- Bottom of opening
- Bottom of opening
- Side (wrong side)
- ½"

(3) Align both sides, right sides together, and sew to the bottom of the opening. Press open the seam allowances.

- Side (wrong side)
- ½"
- Bottom (wrong side)

(4) Align the bottom edges of each side with the bottom piece, right sides together, and sew. Spread the seam allowances toward the bottom.

(6) Pass the cord through from both sides, then knot the ends together.

- RETURN OF HAPPINESS
- 10½"
- 6"

- 1" | 1"
- ½" | (right side)

(5) Turn right side out then create a triple fold with the opening, and stitch in place.

Embroidery Pattern
(actual size)

Use 3 strands, unless noted otherwise.

- French knot, 1 wrap (3866)
- Lazy daisy (3866)
- Center
- Straight, 2 strands (471)
- Outline (471)
- Make split stitches randomly (988) (3346).
- French knot, 2 wraps (3328)
- Back, 2 strands (931)

RETURN

OF HAPPINESS

The Language of Flowers, Lily of the Valley

Thread: DMC embroidery floss No. 25 (471, 645, 841, 844, 932, 988, 3328, 3346, 3347, 3782, 3866); DMC pearl cotton thread No. 5 (471); Art Fiber Endo linen embroidery thread (911)

Fabric: Linen, light blue, 14" x 16"

Other: Fusible interfacing, 14" x 16"; lightweight linen (printed or stamped with text), white, 8" x 8"; double-sided fusible interfacing, 8" x 8"; stamp; kraft tag; string, white; ½"-thick by 1½"-wide wooden frame; small nails or staples (24); bookbinding tape

Finished size: 9¾" x 10¾"

Embroidery Pattern (actual size)

Use 3 strands, unless noted otherwise.

Use No. 25, unless noted otherwise. "#5" denotes No. 5 pearl cotton thread.

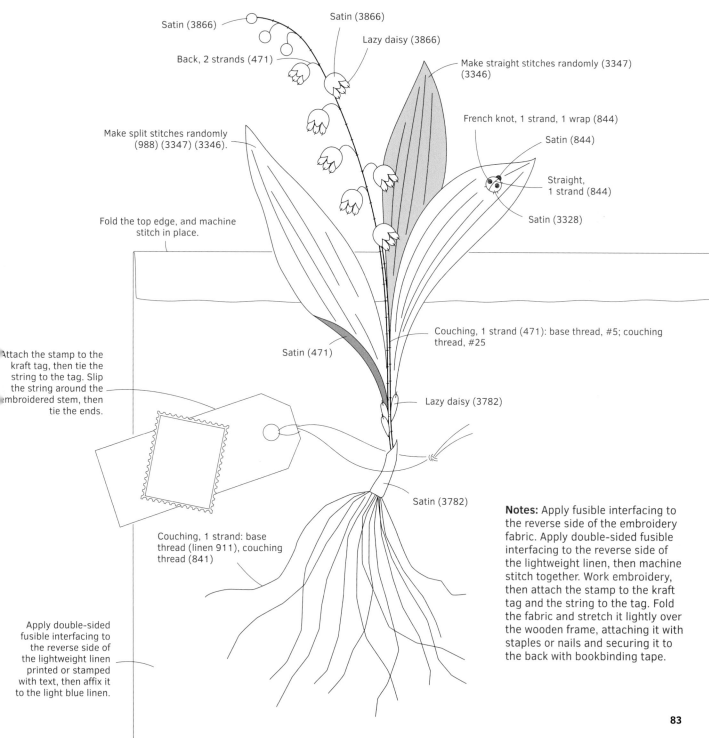

Couching (932): base thread, 2 strands; couching thread, 1 strand

RETURN OF HAPPINESS

Satin (3866)

Satin (3866)

Lazy daisy (3866)

Back, 2 strands (471)

Make straight stitches randomly (3347) (3346)

French knot, 1 strand, 1 wrap (844)

Satin (844)

Make split stitches randomly (988) (3347) (3346).

Straight, 1 strand (844)

Satin (3328)

Fold the top edge, and machine stitch in place.

Couching, 1 strand (471): base thread, #5; couching thread, #25

Attach the stamp to the kraft tag, then tie the string to the tag. Slip the string around the embroidered stem, then tie the ends.

Satin (471)

Lazy daisy (3782)

Satin (3782)

Couching, 1 strand: base thread (linen 911), couching thread (841)

Apply double-sided fusible interfacing to the reverse side of the lightweight linen printed or stamped with text, then affix it to the light blue linen.

Notes: Apply fusible interfacing to the reverse side of the embroidery fabric. Apply double-sided fusible interfacing to the reverse side of the lightweight linen, then machine stitch together. Work embroidery, then attach the stamp to the kraft tag and the string to the tag. Fold the fabric and stretch it lightly over the wooden frame, attaching it with staples or nails and securing it to the back with bookbinding tape.

Gathering White Flowers/White Flower Bag

Thread: DMC embroidery floss No. 25 (988, [470], 522, 729, 935, [934], 3346, [988], 3866); DMC pearl cotton thread No. 8 (3865)

Fabric: Linen, gray, 15¾" x 15¾"; [green (outer fabric), 15¾" x 39½"]

Other: [Linen, mustard (lining), 15¾" x 27½"]; fusible interfacing, 15¾" x 15¾" [15¾" x 31½"]; ½"-wide leather tape, brown, 13¾" x 31½" long, 2 pieces

Finished size: Refer to the diagram.

Notes: Instructions in [brackets] refer to the bag; otherwise, instructions refer to both.

How to Cut the Bag

Apply fusible interfacing to the reverse side of the outer fabric and the bottom fabric before embroidering.

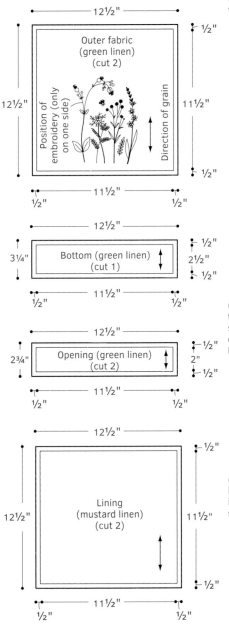

How to Make the Bag

(1) Align the bottom edge of the embroidered outer fabric with the bottom fabric, right sides together, and sew. Spread the seam allowance toward the bottom, turn the project right side out, and stitch the seam allowance in place from the right side.

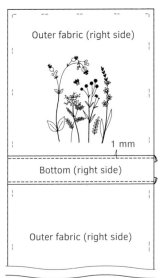

(2) Align the top edge of the lining with the fabric for the opening, right sides together, and sew. Spread the seam allowance toward the opening, and stitch it in place from the right side. Make 2.

(3) Layer the top edges of the outer fabric and lining, with the handles in between as shown in the diagram, and sew. Repeat on the other side.

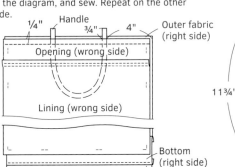

(4) Align the outer fabric with the lining, right sides together, and sew, leaving an opening for turning out. Press the seam allowances open.

(5) Extend the gusset on the bottom edge of the outer fabric, and sew. Cut, leaving a ¼" seam allowance.

(6) As in #5, sew the gusset on the bottom of the lining, then cut seam allowance.

(7) Turn the bag right side out, whipstitch the opening, and fit the lining inside the outer fabric.

(8) Reinforce the handles by machine stitching them.

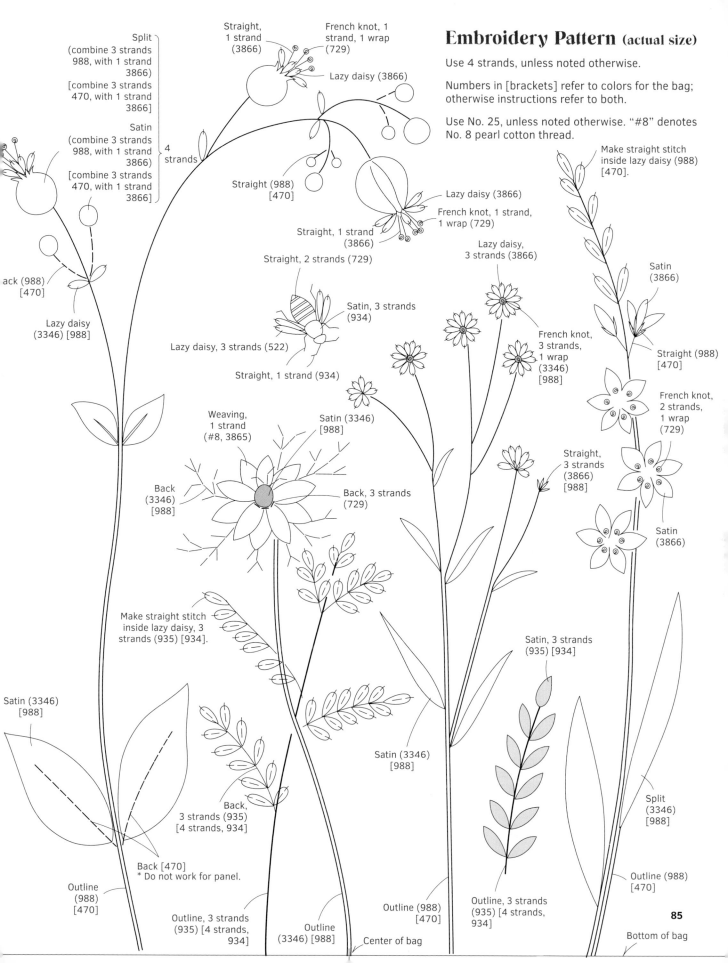

Embroidery Pattern (actual size)

Use 4 strands, unless noted otherwise.

Numbers in [brackets] refer to colors for the bag; otherwise instructions refer to both.

Use No. 25, unless noted otherwise. "#8" denotes No. 8 pearl cotton thread.

Split
(combine 3 strands
988, with 1 strand
3866)
[combine 3 strands
470, with 1 strand
3866]

Satin
(combine 3 strands
988, with 1 strand
3866)
[combine 3 strands
470, with 1 strand
3866]

4 strands

Straight,
1 strand
(3866)

French knot, 1
strand, 1 wrap
(729)

Lazy daisy (3866)

Make straight stitch
inside lazy daisy (988)
[470].

Straight (988)
[470]

Lazy daisy (3866)

French knot, 1 strand,
1 wrap (729)

Straight, 1 strand
(3866)

Straight, 2 strands (729)

Satin, 3 strands
(934)

Lazy daisy,
3 strands (3866)

Satin
(3866)

Straight (988)
[470]

French knot,
3 strands,
1 wrap
(3346)
[988]

French knot,
2 strands,
1 wrap
(729)

ack (988)
[470]

Lazy daisy
(3346) [988]

Lazy daisy, 3 strands (522)

Straight, 1 strand (934)

Straight,
3 strands
(3866)
[988]

Satin
(3866)

Weaving,
1 strand
(#8, 3865)

Satin (3346)
[988]

Back
(3346)
[988]

Back, 3 strands
(729)

Make straight stitch
inside lazy daisy, 3
strands (935) [934].

Satin, 3 strands
(935) [934]

Satin (3346)
[988]

Satin (3346)
[988]

Back,
3 strands (935)
[4 strands, 934]

Split
(3346)
[988]

Back [470]
* Do not work for panel.

Outline
(988)
[470]

Outline, 3 strands
(935) [4 strands,
934]

Outline
(3346) [988]

Outline (988)
[470]

Outline, 3 strands
(935) [4 strands,
934]

Outline (988)
[470]

Center of bag

Bottom of bag

85

In the Rose Garden

Thread: DMC embroidery floss No. 25 (309, 320, 335, 680, 834, 963, 988, 989, 3348, 3363, 3689, 3803, 3821); DMC pearl cotton thread No. 5 (989); Art Fiber Endo linen embroidery thread (116); Mokuba embroidery ribbon No. 1540, 1/8" wide (029, 044, 063, 067)

Fabric: Midweight cotton, white, 9¾" x 23½"

Other: Midweight fusible interfacing, 9¾" x 23½"; floral wire, 22-gauge; paper; quick-drying bond

Finished size: Refer to the diagram.

Notes: Apply fusible interfacing to the reverse side of the embroidery fabric before embroidering. Apply quick-drying bond around the edges of the embroidery on the wrong side; cut out when dry. Attach the floral wire to the reverse side, extend the wire out from the bottom in a circular shape, then attach cut-out rounds of paper above and below the wire with quick-drying bond.

How to Make

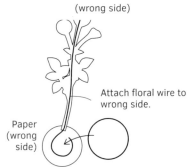

(wrong side)

Attach floral wire to wrong side.

Paper (wrong side)

After cutting out the fabric, use quick-drying bond to attach the floral wire to the stem as shown in the diagram, then attach the cut-out rounds of paper on the top and bottom.

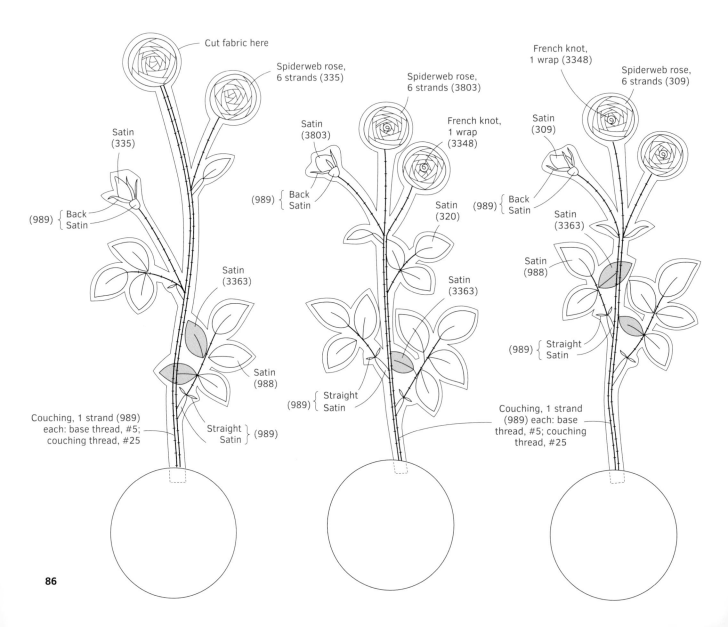

Cut fabric here

Spiderweb rose, 6 strands (335)

Satin (335)

(989) { Back / Satin

Satin (3363)

Satin (988)

Couching, 1 strand (989) each: base thread, #5; couching thread, #25

Straight / Satin } (989)

Spiderweb rose, 6 strands (3803)

Satin (3803)

French knot, 1 wrap (3348)

(989) { Back / Satin

Satin (320)

Satin (3363)

(989) { Straight / Satin

French knot, 1 wrap (3348)

Spiderweb rose, 6 strands (309)

Satin (309)

(989) { Back / Satin

Satin (3363)

Satin (988)

(989) { Straight / Satin

Couching, 1 strand (989) each: base thread, #5; couching thread, #25

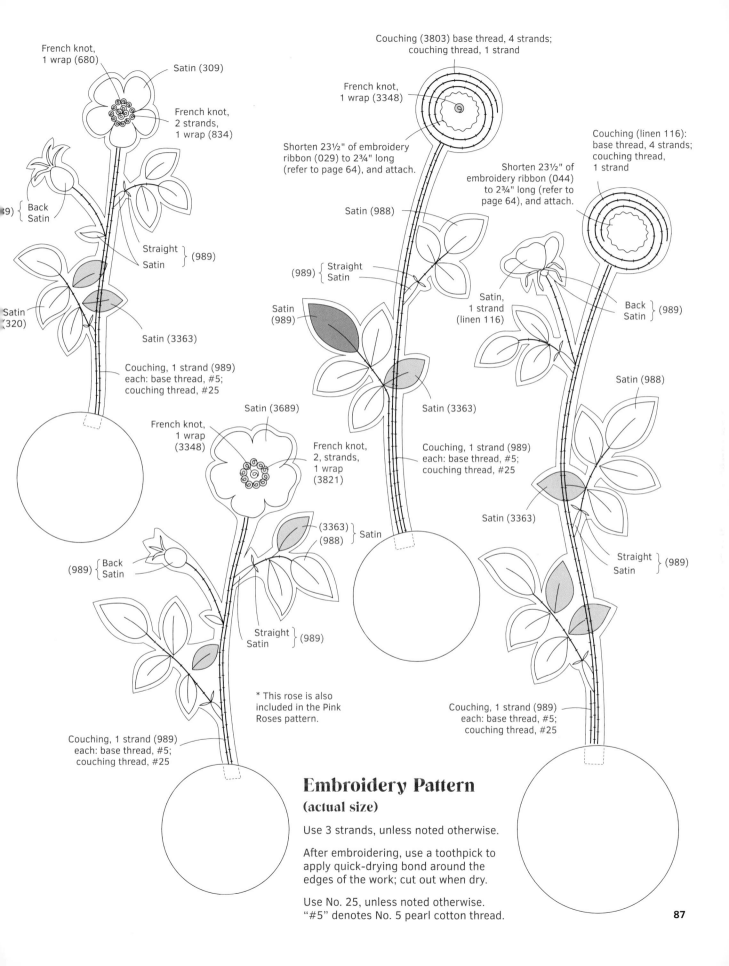

French knot, 1 wrap (680)

Satin (309)

French knot, 2 strands, 1 wrap (834)

Couching (3803) base thread, 4 strands; couching thread, 1 strand

French knot, 1 wrap (3348)

Shorten 23½" of embroidery ribbon (029) to 2¾" long (refer to page 64), and attach.

Couching (linen 116): base thread, 4 strands; couching thread, 1 strand

Shorten 23½" of embroidery ribbon (044) to 2¾" long (refer to page 64), and attach.

9) } Back Satin

Straight } (989)
Satin

Satin (988)

(989) { Straight
        Satin

Satin (988)

Satin, 1 strand (linen 116)

Back } (989)
Satin

Satin (320)

Satin (3363)

Satin (989)

Satin (3363)

Satin (988)

Couching, 1 strand (989) each: base thread, #5; couching thread, #25

French knot, 1 wrap (3348)

Satin (3689)

French knot, 2, strands, 1 wrap (3821)

Couching, 1 strand (989) each: base thread, #5; couching thread, #25

Satin (3363)

Straight } (989)
Satin

(989) { Back
        Satin

(3363) } Satin
(988)

Straight } (989)
Satin

Couching, 1 strand (989) each: base thread, #5; couching thread, #25

Straight } (989)
Satin

* This rose is also included in the Pink Roses pattern.

Couching, 1 strand (989) each: base thread, #5; couching thread, #25

Embroidery Pattern
(actual size)

Use 3 strands, unless noted otherwise.

After embroidering, use a toothpick to apply quick-drying bond around the edges of the work; cut out when dry.

Use No. 25, unless noted otherwise. "#5" denotes No. 5 pearl cotton thread.

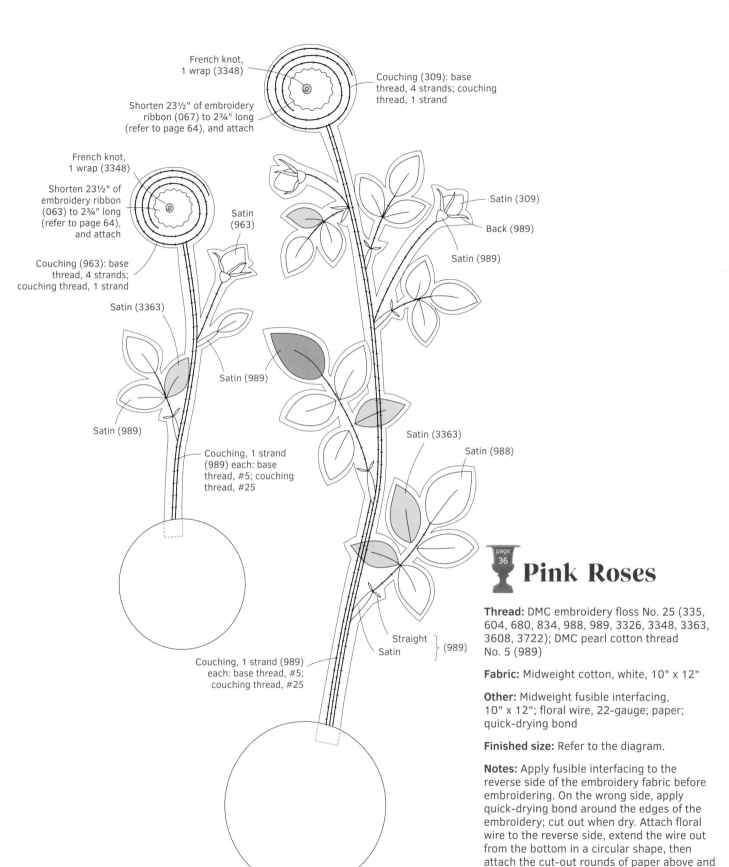

French knot,
1 wrap (3348)

Couching (309): base
thread, 4 strands; couching
thread, 1 strand

Shorten 23½" of embroidery
ribbon (067) to 2¾" long
(refer to page 64), and attach

French knot,
1 wrap (3348)

Satin (309)

Back (989)

Shorten 23½" of
embroidery ribbon
(063) to 2¾" long
(refer to page 64),
and attach

Satin (963)

Satin (989)

Couching (963): base
thread, 4 strands;
couching thread, 1 strand

Satin (3363)

Satin (989)

Satin (989)

Couching, 1 strand
(989) each: base
thread, #5; couching
thread, #25

Satin (3363)

Satin (988)

Straight
Satin } (989)

Couching, 1 strand (989)
each: base thread, #5;
couching thread, #25

page 36 ▾ Pink Roses

Thread: DMC embroidery floss No. 25 (335,
604, 680, 834, 988, 989, 3326, 3348, 3363,
3608, 3722); DMC pearl cotton thread
No. 5 (989)

Fabric: Midweight cotton, white, 10" x 12"

Other: Midweight fusible interfacing,
10" x 12"; floral wire, 22-gauge; paper;
quick-drying bond

Finished size: Refer to the diagram.

Notes: Apply fusible interfacing to the
reverse side of the embroidery fabric before
embroidering. On the wrong side, apply
quick-drying bond around the edges of the
embroidery; cut out when dry. Attach floral
wire to the reverse side, extend the wire out
from the bottom in a circular shape, then
attach the cut-out rounds of paper above and
below the wire with quick-drying bond.

Embroidery Pattern (actual size)

Use 3 strands, unless noted otherwise.

After embroidering, use a toothpick to apply quick-drying bond around the edges of the work; cut out when dry.

Use No. 25, unless noted otherwise. "#5" denotes No. 5 pearl cotton thread.

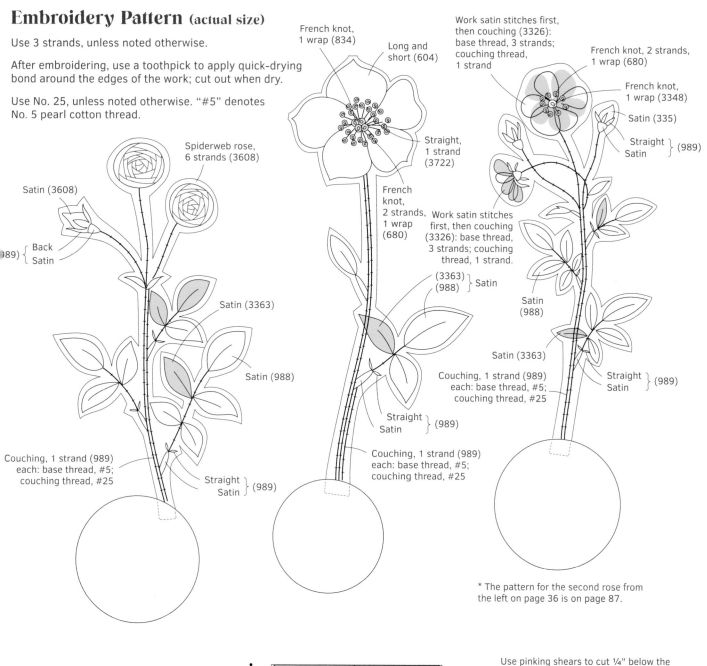

French knot, 1 wrap (834)

Long and short (604)

Spiderweb rose, 6 strands (3608)

Satin (3608)

(989) } Back Satin

Work satin stitches first, then couching (3326): base thread, 3 strands; couching thread, 1 strand

French knot, 2 strands, 1 wrap (680)

French knot, 1 wrap (3348)

Satin (335)

Straight } (989)
Satin

Straight, 1 strand (3722)

French knot, 2 strands, 1 wrap (680)

Work satin stitches first, then couching (3326): base thread, 3 strands; couching thread, 1 strand.

Satin (3363)

(3363) } Satin
(988)

Satin (988)

Satin (988)

Satin (3363)

Couching, 1 strand (989) each: base thread, #5; couching thread, #25

Couching, 1 strand (989) each: base thread, #5; couching thread, #25

Straight } (989)
Satin

Straight } (989)
Satin

Couching, 1 strand (989) each: base thread, #5; couching thread, #25

Straight } (989)
Satin

* The pattern for the second rose from the left on page 36 is on page 87.

How to Cut the Case

Apply fusible interfacing to the reverse side of the outer fabric before embroidering.

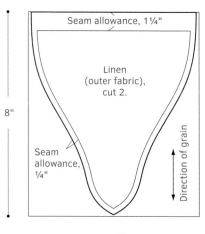

Seam allowance, 1 1/4"

Linen (outer fabric), cut 2.

8"

Seam allowance, 1/4"

Direction of grain

6"

Use pinking shears to cut 1/4" below the top edge of the finished outer fabric.

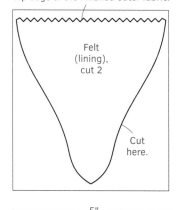

Felt (lining), cut 2

6"

Cut here.

5"

Rose Shears Case

Thread: DMC embroidery floss No. 25 (963, 3346, 3347, 3362); DMC pearl cotton thread No. 5 (3347); Mokuba embroidery ribbon No. 1540, ⅛" wide (063)

Fabric: Linen, blue-gray (outer fabric), 11¾" x 8"

Other: Fusible interfacing, 11¾" x 8"; felt, gray (lining), 10¼" x 6"

Finished size: Refer to the diagram.

Notes: Apply fusible interfacing to the reverse side of the outer fabric before embroidering. Follow instructions to make case. * How to cut diagram on page 89.

Project & Embroidery Patterns
(actual size)

Use 3 strands, unless noted otherwise.

Use No. 25, unless noted otherwise. "#5" denotes No. 5 pearl cotton thread.

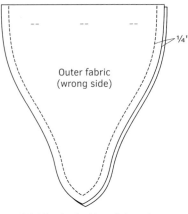

Outer fabric
(wrong side)

¼"

(1) Align both sides of the outer fabric, right sides together, and sew. Press the seam allowances open, and turn the case right side out.

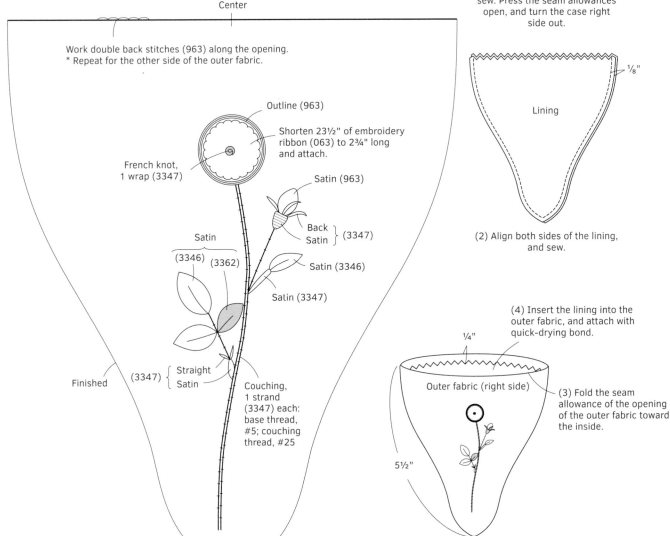

Center

Work double back stitches (963) along the opening.
* Repeat for the other side of the outer fabric.

Outline (963)

Shorten 23½" of embroidery ribbon (063) to 2¾" long and attach.

French knot,
1 wrap (3347)

Satin (963)

Back Satin } (3347)

Satin
(3346) (3362)

Satin (3346)

Satin (3347)

Finished

(3347) { Straight Satin

Couching,
1 strand
(3347) each:
base thread,
#5; couching
thread, #25

Lining

⅛"

(2) Align both sides of the lining, and sew.

(4) Insert the lining into the outer fabric, and attach with quick-drying bond.

¼"

Outer fabric (right side)

(3) Fold the seam allowance of the opening of the outer fabric toward the inside.

5½"

Chamomile

Thread: DMC embroidery floss No. 25 (470, 680, 822, 3347, 3821); DMC pearl cotton thread No. 5 (470)

Fabric: Linen, white, 11¾" x 17¾"

Other: Fusible interfacing, 11¾" x 17¾"; cheesecloth, 2¼" x 6"; text-print fabric, 1½" x 1½"; acrylic paint in white; ⅛"-thick styrene board, 7" x 9¾" bookbinding tape; string, white; letter stamps; inkpad for use on fabric (sepia); kraft tag

Finished size: 7" x 9¾"

Embroidery Pattern (actual size)

Use 3 strands, unless noted otherwise.

Use No. 25, unless noted otherwise. "#5" denotes No. 5 pearl cotton thread.

Using the free-motion function on a sewing machine, machine stitch the other fabrics onto the linen. Paint with acrylic before embroidering, applying paint lightly to the embroidery area.

Cheesecloth

Lazy daisy (470)

French knot, 2 wraps (470)

French knot, { (680)
1 wrap { (3821)

Back (470)

Lazy daisy (822)

Straight (822)

Straight (470)

Lazy daisy (470)

Notes: Apply fusible interfacing to the reverse side of the embroidery fabric. Using the free-motion function on a sewing machine, machine stitch together. Machine stitch the cheesecloth and the text-print fabric onto the white linen, then lightly paint the entire piece with acrylic. When dry, embroider the pattern. Stamp the lettering on the kraft tag, then attach the string to the tag. Fold the fabric around the edges of the styrene board and secure it to the back with bookbinding tape.

Straight (3347)

Back (3347)

Text-print fabric

Stamp lettering on the kraft tag, then tie the string to the tag, slip the string around the embroidered stem, and tie the ends.

Chamomile

Stamp.

Couching, 1 strand (470) each: base thread, #5; couching thread, #25

91

Herb Wreath Bag

Thread: DMC embroidery floss No. 25 (3799)

Fabric: Linen, gray, 31½" x 35½"

Other: Fusible interfacing, 31½" x 35½"; leather, black, 4¾" x 2", 2 pieces; ¼"-diameter handle cording, 11" long, 2 pieces; bottom plate, 11" x 3"

Finished size: Refer to the diagram.

Notes: Apply fusible interfacing to the reverse side of the outer fabric before embroidering. Follow the instructions to make the bag.

How to Cut the Bag

Finish the ends of the seam allowances with a zigzag machine stitch.

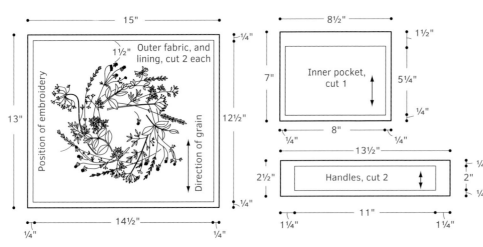

Outer fabric, and lining, cut 2 each

Position of embroidery · Direction of grain

15" · 1½" · 13" · 12½" · 14½" · ¼"

Inner pocket, cut 1

8½" · 1½" · 7" · 5¼" · 8" · ¼" · 2½"

Handles, cut 2

13½" · ¼" · 2" · ¼" · 11" · 1¼"

How to Make the Bag

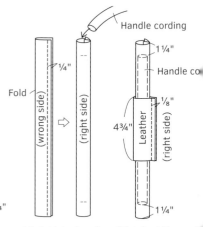

Handle cording · Handle cording · Leather

Fold (wrong side) · (right side) · (right side) · ¼" · 1¼" · ⅛" · 4¾" · 1¼"

(1) Fold the handle fabric in half and sew the edges together. Turn the handle right side out and insert the cording.

(2) Adjust the cord[ing] [at] the center of the ha[ndle]. Wrap the middle of [the] handle with leather, sew the edges toge[ther]. Make 2.

(10) Reinforce the opening by machi[ne] stitching all aroun[d].

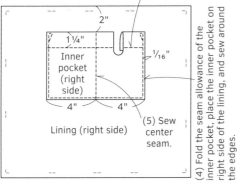

(3) Fold the seam allowance at the opening for the inner pocket and sew it in place.

Inner pocket (right side) · Lining (right side) · 2" · 1¼" · ¹⁄₁₆" · 4" · 4"

(4) Fold the seam allowance of the inner pocket, place the inner pocket on right side of the lining, and sew around the edges.

(5) Sew center seam

(7) Layer the outer fabrics and linings, right sides together, and sew the sides and bottom edges together, leaving an opening for turning out. Press the seam allowances open.

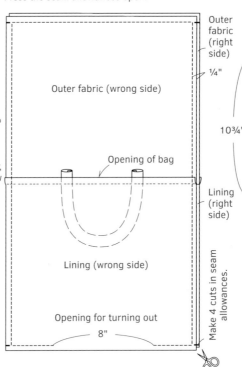

Outer fabric (right side) · ¼" · Outer fabric (wrong side) · Opening of bag · Lining (right side) · 10¾" · Lining (wrong side) · Make 4 cuts in seam allowances. · Opening for turning out · 8"

(6) Layer the outer fabric and lining, right sides together, with the handle in between as shown in the diagram; sew top edges together. Repeat for the other side.

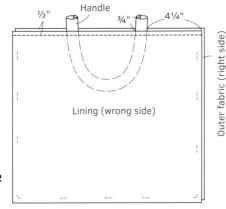

Handle · ½" · ¾" · 4¼" · Lining (wrong side) · Outer fabric (right side)

Outer fabric (right side) · ⅛" · 11" · 3¼"

(9) Turn right side out, whipstitch the opening, and fit the lining inside the outer fabric.

(8) Extend the gusset on the bottom and sew together. Cut, leaving a ¼" seam allowance.

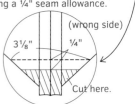

(wrong side) · 3⅛" · ¼" · Cut here.

92

Embroidery Pattern (enlarge by 125%)

Use 2 strands (3799) for all stitches.

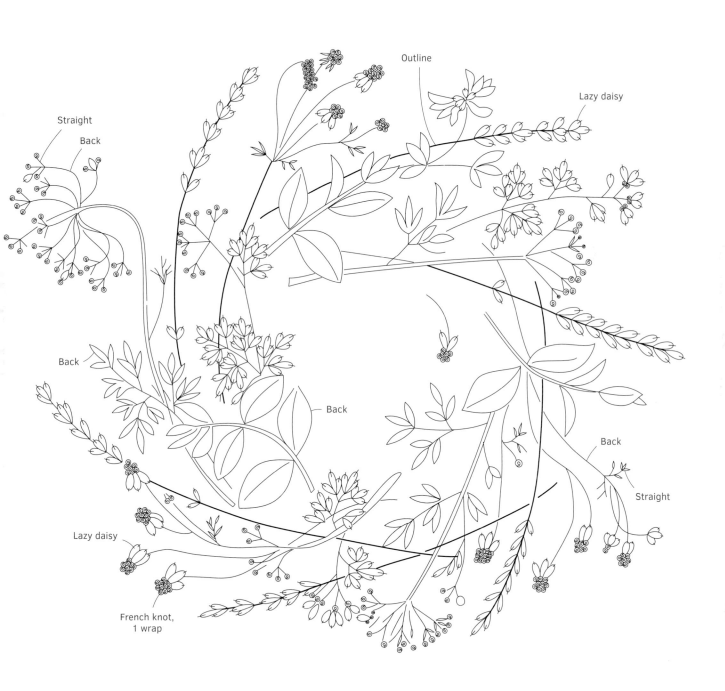

Outline

Lazy daisy

Straight

Back

Back

Back

Back

Straight

Lazy daisy

French knot,
1 wrap

Berry Labels

Thread: DMC embroidery floss No. 25 (326, 347, 729, 777, 823, 3012, 3328, 3346, 3347, 3364, 3807, 3838, 3866)

Fabric: Linen, unbleached, 4¾" x 4¼" for each

Other: Fusible interfacing, 2¼" x 4¼" for each; linen string; 5-mm-diameter eyelet; letter stamps; inkpad for use on fabric (sepia)

Finished size: Refer to the diagram.

Notes: Apply fusible interfacing to the reverse side of the embroidery fabric before embroidering. Stamp the lettering. Make the label and attach the eyelet. Pass linen string through and tie the ends.

(6) Pass linen string through and tie the ends.

(5) Attach the eyelet.

½"   ⅛"

(1) Apply the fusible interfacing to the reverse side before embroidering.

(4) Layer the linen fabric, wrong sides together, and sew around the edges.

(3) Cut out the fabric. Cut another piece in the same size.

Wild Strawberry

(2) Stamp the lettering.

Embroidery Pattern (actual size)

Use 3 strands, unless noted otherwise.

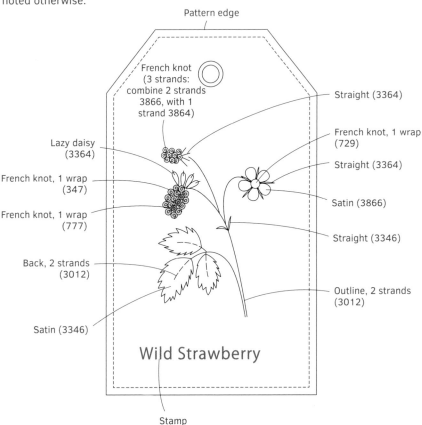

Pattern edge

French knot (3 strands: combine 2 strands 3866, with 1 strand 3864)

Lazy daisy (3364)

French knot, 1 wrap (347)

French knot, 1 wrap (777)

Back, 2 strands (3012)

Satin (3346)

Straight (3364)

French knot, 1 wrap (729)

Straight (3364)

Satin (3866)

Straight (3346)

Outline, 2 strands (3012)

Wild Strawberry

Stamp

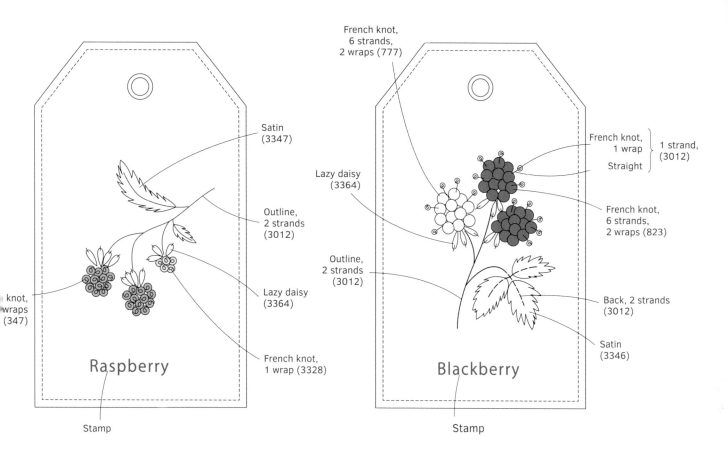

Raspberry

Satin (3347)

Outline, 2 strands (3012)

Lazy daisy (3364)

French knot, 1 wrap (3328)

knot, wraps (347)

Stamp

Blackberry

French knot, 6 strands, 2 wraps (777)

French knot, 1 wrap / Straight } 1 strand, (3012)

French knot, 6 strands, 2 wraps (823)

Lazy daisy (3364)

Outline, 2 strands (3012)

Back, 2 strands (3012)

Satin (3346)

Stamp

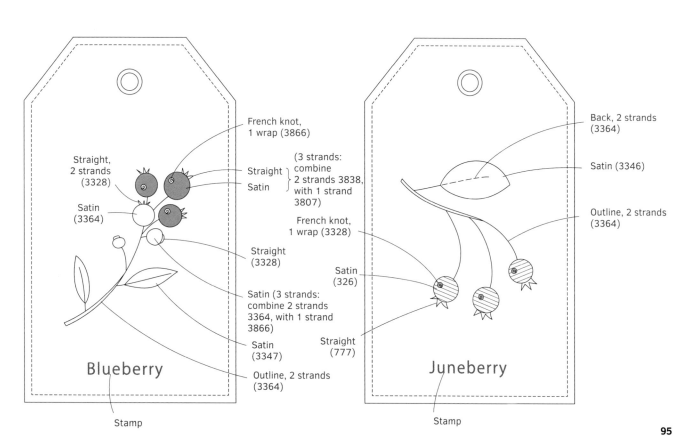

Blueberry

French knot, 1 wrap (3866)

Straight, 2 strands (3328)

Straight
Satin } (3 strands: combine 2 strands 3838, with 1 strand 3807)

Satin (3364)

Straight (3328)

French knot, 1 wrap (3328)

Satin (3 strands: combine 2 strands 3364, with 1 strand 3866)

Satin (3347)

Outline, 2 strands (3364)

Stamp

Juneberry

Back, 2 strands (3364)

Satin (3346)

Outline, 2 strands (3364)

Satin (326)

Straight (777)

Stamp

95

Berry Kiss Lock Purse

Thread: DMC embroidery floss No. 25 (347, 729, 3346, 3347, 3866); DMC pearl cotton thread No. 5 (336)

Fabric: Linen, unbleached (outer fabric), 6" x 11¾"

Other: Fusible interfacing, 6" x 11¾"; striped cotton (lining), 6" x 11¾"; tie-dyed cloth, green; double-sided fusible interfacing; seed beads, dark brown (larger), red (smaller); 3¼"-wide clasp, silver; paper string; quick-drying bond

Finished size: Refer to the diagram.

Notes: Apply fusible interfacing to the reverse side of the outer fabric before embroidering. Follow instructions to make the kiss lock purse, then make the tassel and attach it to the purse.

How to Cut the Purse

Apply fusible interfacing to the reverse side of the outer fabric before embroidering, then cut.

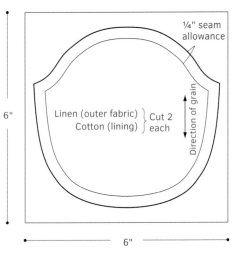

¼" seam allowance

6"

Linen (outer fabric)
Cotton (lining) } Cut 2 each

Direction of grain

6"

Outer fabric (right side)

¼"

Lining (wrong side)

(1) Layer the outer fabric and lining, right sides together, and sew along the edge of the opening. Repeat for the other set of outer fabric and lining.

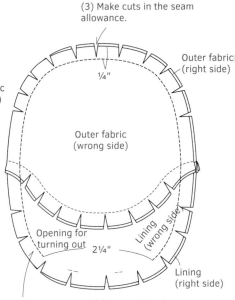

(3) Make cuts in the seam allowance.

¼"

Outer fabric (right side)

Outer fabric (wrong side)

Opening for turning out   2¼"

Lining (wrong side)

Lining (right side)

(2) Layer 2 sets of fabric, right sides together, and sew, leaving an opening for turning out.

Lining (right side)

Paper string

(5) Whipstitch the paper string along the opening edge.

Outer fabric (right side)

(4) Turn the purse right side out, whipstitch the opening, and fit the lining inside the outer fabric.

(6) Apply quick-drying bond to channel of clasp and use an eyeleteer to push the lining inside. Use pliers to bend the corners back firmly.

(7) Make and attach the tassel.

3¾"

How to Make the Tassel

Use No. 5 (336)

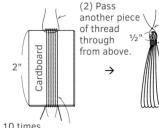

2"

Cardboard

Wrap 10 times.

(1) Wrap the embroidery thread (as is, 6-stranded from skein) around a piece of cardboard.

(2) Pass another piece of thread through from above.

½"

(3) Slide the thread off the cardboard and tie it tightly with thread from (2).

(4) Wrap the bundle of threads with another piece of thread. Tie the ends together and hide the knot inside the tassel.

1¼"

(6) Twist these 2 threads together, make a loop, and tuck them inside the tassel.

(5) Trim the tassel ends and untangle the threads.

Front

Satin, 4 strands (3866)

French knot, 1wrap (729)

Satin, 1 strand, #5 (336)

Tie-dyed fabric for leaves

Machine stitch onto linen.

Pattern edge

Lazy daisy, 4 strands (3346)

Work French knot stitches, 4 strands, 1 wrap (347), then add 5 red beads to balance out the fullness.

Fill in with small red beads.

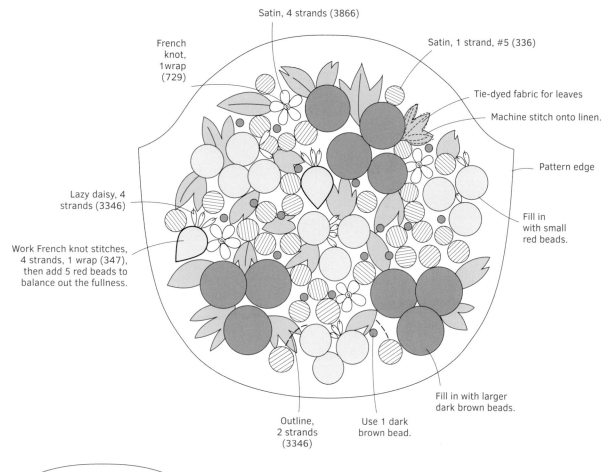

Outline, 2 strands (3346)

Use 1 dark brown bead.

Fill in with larger dark brown beads.

Back

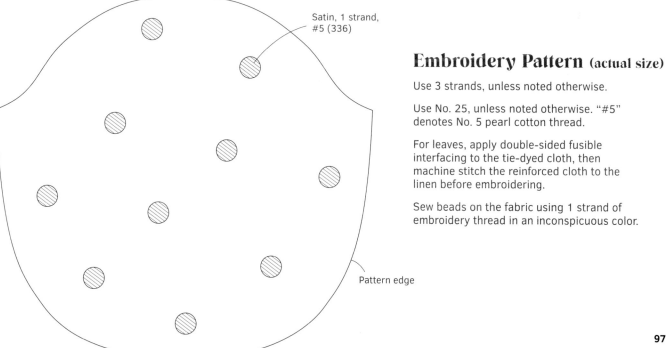

Satin, 1 strand, #5 (336)

Pattern edge

Embroidery Pattern (actual size)

Use 3 strands, unless noted otherwise.

Use No. 25, unless noted otherwise. "#5" denotes No. 5 pearl cotton thread.

For leaves, apply double-sided fusible interfacing to the tie-dyed cloth, then machine stitch the reinforced cloth to the linen before embroidering.

Sew beads on the fabric using 1 strand of embroidery thread in an inconspicuous color.

Autumn Hydrangea Book Cover

Thread: DMC embroidery floss No. 25 (31, 320, 793); Art Fiber Endo linen embroidery thread (207)

Fabric: Linen, dark gray, 17¾" x 8"

Other: Fusible interfacing, 17¾" x 8"; ¾"-wide grosgrain ribbon, purple, 7" long; ⅛"-wide ribbon, purple, 9¾" long

Finished size: Refer to the diagram.

Note: This is for a standard Japanese paperback, which is smaller than traditional American formats. Apply fusible interfacing to the reverse side of the embroidery fabric before embroidering. Follow the instructions to make the book cover.

How to Cut the Book Cover

Apply fusible interfacing to the reverse side of the fabric before embroidering, then finish the edges with a zigzag machine stitch.

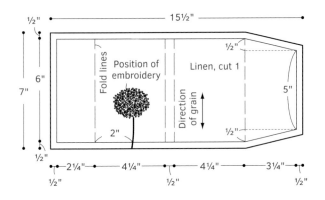

How to Make the Book Cover

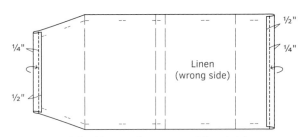

(1) Fold seam allowances on left and right toward wrong side and sew in place

Embroidery Pattern (actual size)

Lazy daisy (4 strands: combine 2 strands 320, with 1 strand 793 & 1 strand 31)

French knot, 1 strand, 1 wrap (linen 207)

French knot, 3 strands, 1 wrap (31)

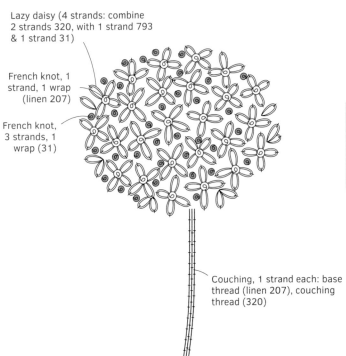

Couching, 1 strand each: base thread (linen 207), couching thread (320)

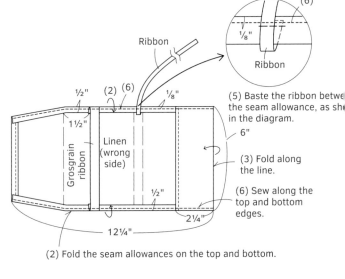

Ribbon

(5) Baste the ribbon between the seam allowance, as sh[ow]n in the diagram.

(3) Fold along the line.

(6) Sew along the top and bottom edges.

(2) Fold the seam allowances on the top and bottom.

(4) Fold under ½" at the ends of the grosgrain ribbon and baste the ribbon in place at the top and bottom.

Autumn Brooches * Patterns in photo, from left to right, A, B, C, D

Thread
A: DMC embroidery floss No. 25 (350, 921, 3828)
B: DMC embroidery floss No. 25 (779, 938, 3830), DMC pearl cotton thread No. 8 (902)
C: DMC embroidery floss No. 25 (3828, 4130)
D: DMC embroidery floss No. 25 (779, 921, 938, 3821)

Fabric
B, D: Linen, dark brown, 3" x 3" for each
A, C: Midweight cotton, white, 4" x 4" for each

Fusible interfacing
B, D: 3" x 3" for each
A, C: 4" x 4" for each

Felt
B, D: dark brown, 2¼" x 2¼" for each
A, C: light brown, 2" x 2¼" for each

Other: brooch pin; quick-drying bond; button base: B, 1¾" diameter; D, 1¼" diameter

Finished size: Refer to the diagram.

Notes: Apply the fusible interfacing to the reverse side of the embroidery fabric before embroidering. Embroidered chain stitches continue off the fabric to create stems. Follow the instructions to make the brooch.

How to Make the Brooches   B, D

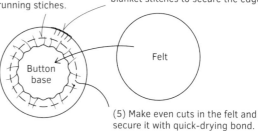

(3) Insert the button base and gather the fabric around it with running stiches.

(4) Looking at the wrong side, work blanket stitches to secure the edge.

Button base

Felt

(5) Make even cuts in the felt and secure it with quick-drying bond.

(6) Cut out a ¼" x ½" piece of felt. Attach the brooch pin to the back and cover it with felt.

⅛"

¼"

(2) Make running stitches.

(1) After embroidering, cut out the pattern, leaving a ¼" seam allowance around edge.

Embroidery Patterns
(actual size)

Use 3 strands, unless noted otherwise.

Use No. 25, unless noted otherwise. "#8" denotes No. 8 pearl cotton thread.

A, C

(wrong side)

(1) After embroidering, cut out the pattern, then make chevron shapes around the edge, fold the fabric to the back, and secure it with quick-drying bond.

(2) Cut felt to the same size and attach with quick-drying bond (for C, make holes).

(3) Cut out a ¼" x ½" piece of felt. Attach a brooch pin to the back, and cover with felt.

A

Back (3828)

Split (3 strands: combine 2 strands 350, with 1 strand 921)

Back (350)

Continuing from the back stitches, work chain stitches off fabric, 4 strands (3828).

B

When finishing, work blanket stitches, 4 strands (779).

Weaving, #8 (902)

Satin (938)

French knot, 1 wrap (3830)

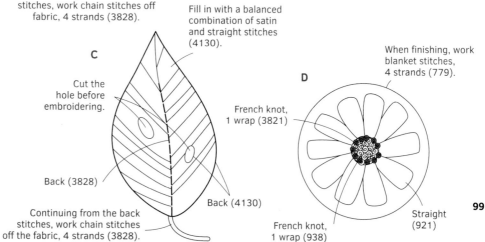

Fill in with a balanced combination of satin and straight stitches (4130).

C

Cut the hole before embroidering.

Back (3828)

Back (4130)

Continuing from the back stitches, work chain stitches off the fabric, 4 strands (3828).

D

When finishing, work blanket stitches, 4 strands (779).

French knot, 1 wrap (3821)

Straight (921)

French knot, 1 wrap (938)

Autumn Bouquet

Thread: DMC embroidery floss No. 25 (27, 151, 153, 340, 471, 727, 758, 3012, 3346, 3347, 3348, 3350, 3712, 3727, 3803, 3821, 3860); DMC pearl cotton thread No. 5 (3012, 3347, 3350); Art Fiber Endo linen embroidery thread (102)

Fabric: Linen, white, 31½" x 21½" (embroidery fabric)

Other: Linen, gray (for the base), 31½" x 13¾"; fusible interfacing, 31½" x 21½"; double-sided fusible interfacing, 13¾" x 9¾"; tulle, moss green; 1"-wide linen tape, 13¾" long

Finished size: Refer to the diagram.

Notes: Apply the fusible interfacing to the reverse side of the designated fabric before embroidering. Follow the instructions to make it look like a book.

How to Cut

Apply the fusible interfacing to the reverse side of the embroidery fabric and to the reverse side of the finished area of Base 1.

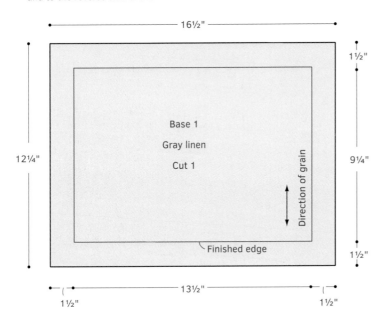

Apply double-sided fusible interfacing to the reverse side of Base 2.

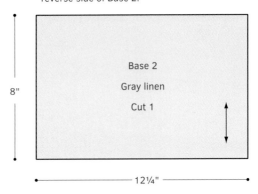

Work embroidery on 1 piece, apply quick-drying bond around the edges of the work; cut when dry.

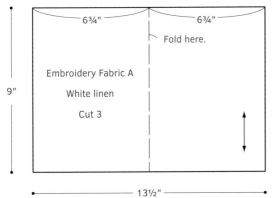

Work embroidery, apply quick-drying bond around the edges of the work, and then cut.

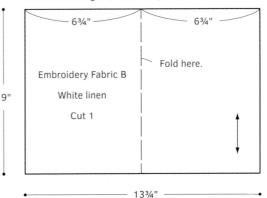

How to Make

(1) Work embroidery on Embroidery Fabric A & B. Apply quick-drying bond to the finished edges to prevent fraying, and when dry, cut out as shown in the diagrams.

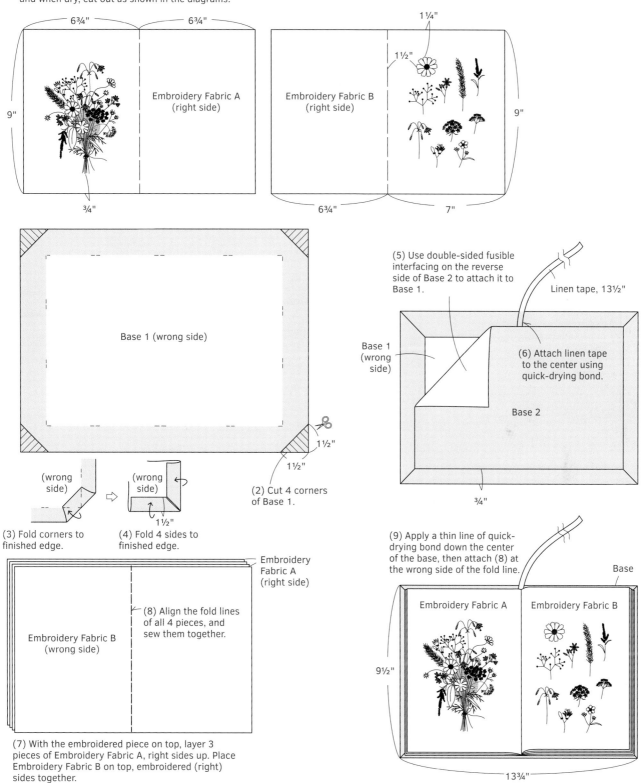

6¾" 6¾"

Embroidery Fabric A
(right side)

9"

¾"

1¼"

1½"

Embroidery Fabric B
(right side)

9"

6¾" 7"

Base 1 (wrong side)

1½"

1½"

(2) Cut 4 corners
of Base 1.

(wrong
side)

⇨

(wrong
side)

1½"

(3) Fold corners to
finished edge.

(4) Fold 4 sides to
finished edge.

(5) Use double-sided fusible
interfacing on the reverse
side of Base 2 to attach it to
Base 1.

Linen tape, 13½"

Base 1
(wrong
side)

(6) Attach linen tape
to the center using
quick-drying bond.

Base 2

¾"

Embroidery
Fabric A
(right side)

(8) Align the fold lines
of all 4 pieces, and
sew them together.

Embroidery Fabric B
(wrong side)

(7) With the embroidered piece on top, layer 3
pieces of Embroidery Fabric A, right sides up. Place
Embroidery Fabric B on top, embroidered (right)
sides together.

(9) Apply a thin line of quick-
drying bond down the center
of the base, then attach (8) at
the wrong side of the fold line.

Base

Embroidery Fabric A

Embroidery Fabric B

9½"

13¾"

Embroidery Pattern (actual size)

Use 3 strands, unless noted otherwise.

Use No. 25, unless noted otherwise. "#5" denotes No. 5 pearl cotton thread.

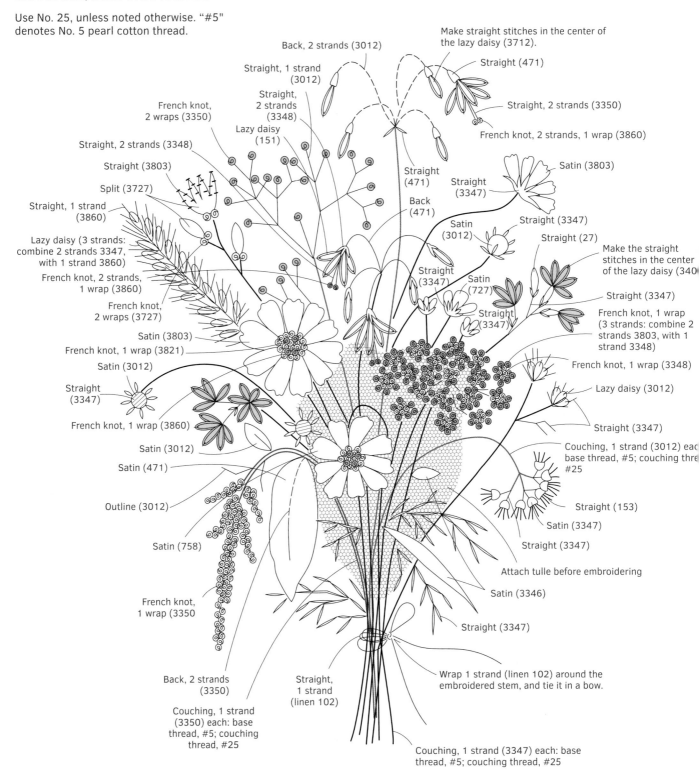

Back, 2 strands (3012)

Straight, 1 strand (3012)

Straight, 2 strands (3348)

French knot, 2 wraps (3350)

Lazy daisy (151)

Straight, 2 strands (3348)

Straight (3803)

Split (3727)

Straight, 1 strand (3860)

Lazy daisy (3 strands: combine 2 strands 3347, with 1 strand 3860)

French knot, 2 strands, 1 wrap (3860)

French knot, 2 wraps (3727)

Satin (3803)

French knot, 1 wrap (3821)

Satin (3012)

Straight (3347)

French knot, 1 wrap (3860)

Satin (3012)

Satin (471)

Outline (3012)

Satin (758)

French knot, 1 wrap (3350

Back, 2 strands (3350)

Couching, 1 strand (3350) each: base thread, #5; couching thread, #25

Straight, 1 strand (linen 102)

Make straight stitches in the center of the lazy daisy (3712).

Straight (471)

Straight, 2 strands (3350)

French knot, 2 strands, 1 wrap (3860)

Satin (3803)

Straight (3347)

Straight (3347)

Straight (27)

Make the straight stitches in the center of the lazy daisy (340

Straight (3347)

French knot, 1 wrap (3 strands: combine 2 strands 3803, with 1 strand 3348)

French knot, 1 wrap (3348)

Lazy daisy (3012)

Straight (3347)

Couching, 1 strand (3012) eac base thread, #5; couching thre #25

Straight (153)

Satin (3347)

Straight (3347)

Attach tulle before embroidering

Satin (3346)

Straight (3347)

Wrap 1 strand (linen 102) around the embroidered stem, and tie it in a bow.

Straight (471)

Back (471)

Satin (3012)

Straight (3347)

Satin (727)

Straight (3347)

Couching, 1 strand (3347) each: base thread, #5; couching thread, #25

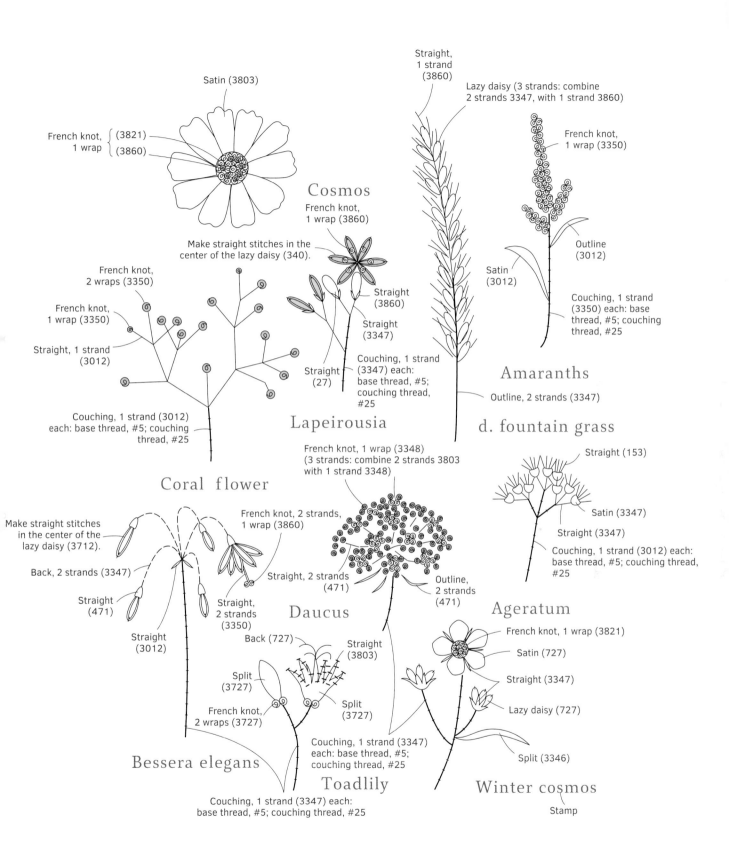

Satin (3803)

French knot,
1 wrap { (3821)
         (3860)

Cosmos

French knot,
1 wrap (3860)

Make straight stitches in the
center of the lazy daisy (340).

Straight
(3860)

Straight
(3347)

Straight
(27)

Couching, 1 strand
(3347) each:
base thread, #5;
couching thread,
#25

Lapeirousia

French knot,
2 wraps (3350)

French knot,
1 wrap (3350)

Straight, 1 strand
(3012)

Couching, 1 strand (3012)
each: base thread, #5; couching
thread, #25

Coral flower

Make straight stitches
in the center of the
lazy daisy (3712).

Back, 2 strands (3347)

Straight
(471)

Straight
(3012)

Straight,
2 strands
(3350)

French knot, 2 strands,
1 wrap (3860)

Straight, 2 strands
(471)

French knot, 1 wrap (3348)
(3 strands: combine 2 strands 3803
with 1 strand 3348)

Outline,
2 strands
(471)

Daucus

Back (727)

Straight
(3803)

Split
(3727)

Split
(3727)

French knot,
2 wraps (3727)

Couching, 1 strand (3347)
each: base thread, #5;
couching thread, #25

Bessera elegans

Toadlily

Couching, 1 strand (3347) each:
base thread, #5; couching thread, #25

Straight,
1 strand
(3860)

Lazy daisy (3 strands: combine
2 strands 3347, with 1 strand 3860)

French knot,
1 wrap (3350)

Outline
(3012)

Satin
(3012)

Couching, 1 strand
(3350) each: base
thread, #5; couching
thread, #25

Amaranths

Outline, 2 strands (3347)

d. fountain grass

Straight (153)

Satin (3347)

Straight (3347)

Couching, 1 strand (3012) each:
base thread, #5; couching thread,
#25

Ageratum

French knot, 1 wrap (3821)

Satin (727)

Straight (3347)

Lazy daisy (727)

Split (3346)

Winter cosmos

Stamp

103

Dusty Miller Mini Bag

Thread: DMC embroidery floss No. 25 (169, 928)

Fabric: Linen, brown, 8" x 9¾"

Other: Fusible interfacing, 8" x 9¾"; felt, gray, 8" x 6"; 3-mm leather cord, brown, 9¾" long

Finished size: Refer to the diagram.

Notes: Apply fusible interfacing to the reverse side of the linen before embroidering. Follow the instructions to make the mini bag.

How to Cut the Bag

Embroidery Pattern (actual size)

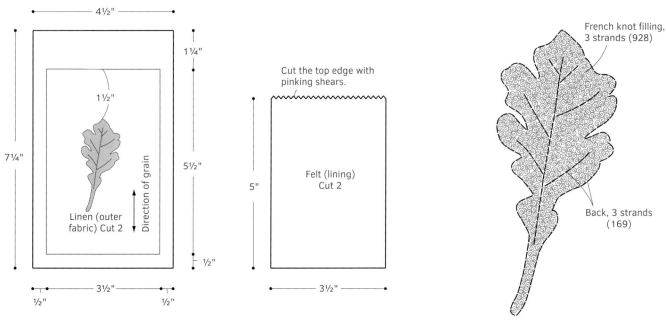

4½"

1¼"

1½"

7¼"

5½"

Direction of grain

Linen (outer fabric) Cut 2

½"

3½"

½" ½"

Cut the top edge with pinking shears.

5"

Felt (lining)
Cut 2

3½"

French knot filling, 3 strands (928)

Back, 3 strands (169)

How to Make the Bag

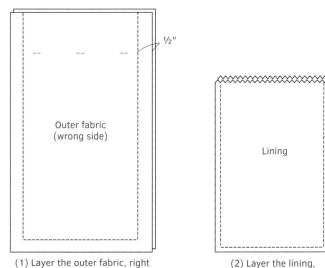

½"

Outer fabric
(wrong side)

(1) Layer the outer fabric, right sides together, and sew. Press the seam allowances open, and turn right side out.

Lining

¼"

(2) Layer the lining, and sew.

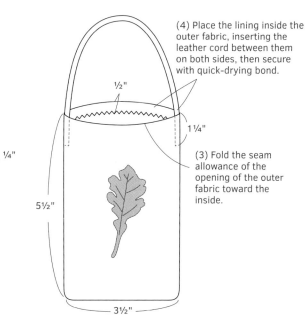

(4) Place the lining inside the outer fabric, inserting the leather cord between them on both sides, then secure with quick-drying bond.

½"

1¼"

(3) Fold the seam allowance of the opening of the outer fabric toward the inside.

5½"

3½"

Winter Panel

Thread: DMC embroidery floss No. 25 (169, 327, 367, 368, 503, 822, 841, 928, 3041, 3053, 3347, 3348, 3828, 3865); DMC pearl cotton thread No. 5 (368, 3053); DMC pearl cotton thread No. 8 (3865); Art Fiber Endo linen embroidery thread (297, 911)

Fabric: Linen, white, 17¾" x 15¾"

Other: Fusible interfacing, 17¾" x 15¾"; double-sided fusible interfacing, 17¾" x 15¾"; linen, purple, 17¾" x 15¾"; linen, beige, 2¼" x 2½"; invisible thread; organdy ribbon, beige, ¼" wide; 2-mm-thick styrene board, 13¼" x 10¼"; bookbinding tape; letter stamps; inkpad for use on fabric (sepia); wire; black pen; quick-drying bond

Finished size: 13¼" x 10¼"

Notes: Apply fusible interfacing to the reverse side of the white linen. Cut the purple linen in an L shape, apply double-sided fusible interfacing to the reverse side, and attach it to the white linen. Attach white #8 thread (3865) along the border of the white linen, securing it with couching stitches. Embroider the pattern. Stamp the lettering on the beige linen, then attach it with the wire. Sew the organdy ribbon in place. Mount the fabric on the styrene board by folding the fabric around the edges and securing it to the back with bookbinding tape.

How to Cut

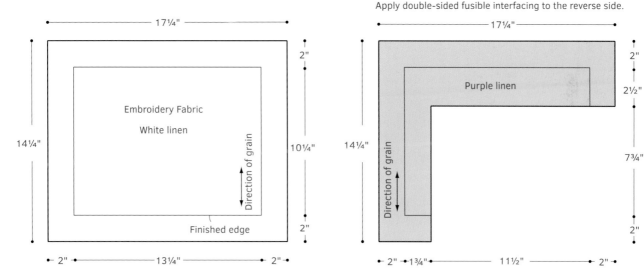

How to Make the Panel

(1) With the double-sided fusible interfacing, attach the purple linen on top of the embroidery fabric (that has fusible interfacing on its reverse side).

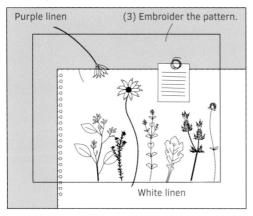

(2) Attach #8 thread (3865) along the edge of the fabric and secure it with couching stitches, using 1 strand of #25 embroidery thread in same color.

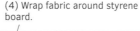

(4) Wrap fabric around styrene board.

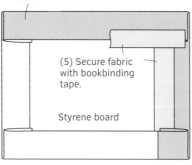

(5) Secure fabric with bookbinding tape.

Styrene board

Embroidery Pattern
(actual size)

Use 3 strands, unless noted otherwise.

Use No. 25, unless noted otherwise. "#5" denotes No. 5 pearl cotton thread, and "#8" denotes No. 8 pearl cotton thread.

Attach #8 thread (3865) along border between the white and purple linen, and use 1 strand of #25 (3865) to secure it with couching stitches.

* Try not to work couching stitches on purple linen.

Couching, 1 strand (368) each: base thread, #5; couching thread, #25

Matchmark ▼

Straight (368)

Split (822)

Split (822)

Straight (368)

Satin (3041)

Straight (368)

French knot, 1 wrap (3 strands: combine 2 strands 3828, with 1 strand 368)

Back (368)

Straight (3348)

French knot, 1 wrap (822)

Satin, 1 strand (linen 207)

Straight (367)

Couching, 1 strand each: base thread (linen 911); couching thread, #25 (841)

Couching, 1 strand (368) each: base thread, #5; couching thread, #25

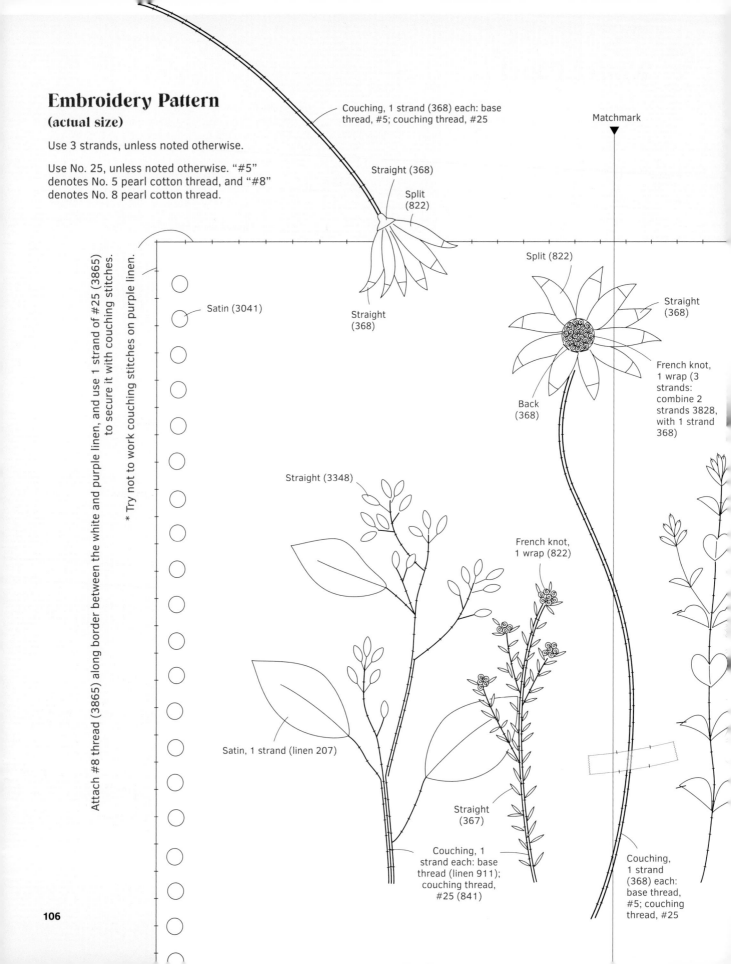

106

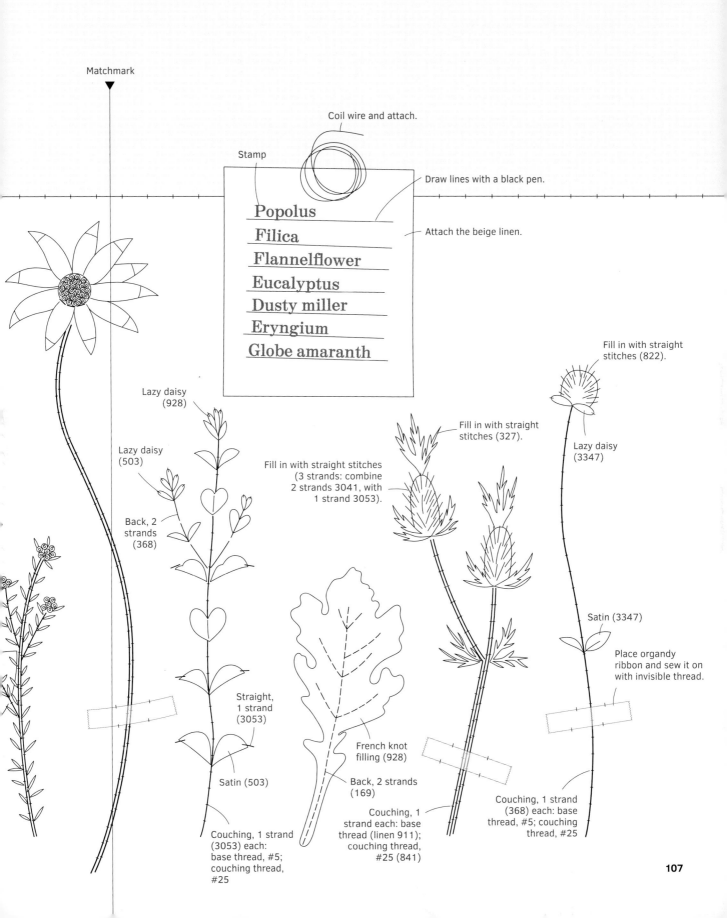

Matchmark

Coil wire and attach.

Stamp

Draw lines with a black pen.

Popolus
Filica
Flannelflower
Eucalyptus
Dusty miller
Eryngium
Globe amaranth

Attach the beige linen.

Fill in with straight stitches (822).

Lazy daisy (928)

Fill in with straight stitches (327).

Lazy daisy (3347)

Lazy daisy (503)

Fill in with straight stitches (3 strands: combine 2 strands 3041, with 1 strand 3053).

Back, 2 strands (368)

Satin (3347)

Place organdy ribbon and sew it on with invisible thread.

Straight, 1 strand (3053)

French knot filling (928)

Satin (503)

Back, 2 strands (169)

Couching, 1 strand (368) each: base thread, #5; couching thread, #25

Couching, 1 strand (3053) each: base thread, #5; couching thread, #25

Couching, 1 strand each: base thread (linen 911); couching thread, #25 (841)

 # Framed Flower Jugs

Thread: DMC embroidery floss No. 25
Large: (640, 3862, 3866); Art Fiber Endo linen
embroidery thread to match color of fabric.
Medium: (640, 642, 729, 3821, 3862)
Small: (844)

Fabric
Large: Linen, checked, 10" x 10"
Medium: Linen, striped, 9" x 9"
Small: linen, woven, 8" x 8"

Other
Large: Fusible interfacing, 10" x 10"; linen, light blue,
4" x 4"; double-sided fusible interfacing, 4" x 4"; tulle,
moss green; 6"-diameter embroidery hoop; ladybug
charm, 1 piece; invisible thread; quick-drying bond
Medium: Fusible interfacing, 9" x 9"; tulle, moss green;
5"-diameter embroidery hoop; bee charms, 3 pieces;
invisible thread; quick-drying bond
Small: Fusible interfacing, 8" x 8"; lead sheet;
annealing wire (for jug handle and base); 4"-diameter
embroidery hoop; snowflake charm, 1 piece; quick-
drying bond

Finished size: Refer to the diagram.

Small

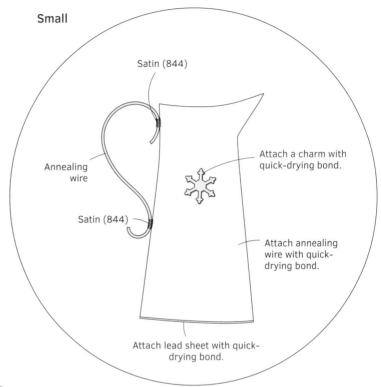

Satin (844)

Annealing
wire

Satin (844)

Attach a charm with
quick-drying bond.

Attach annealing
wire with quick-
drying bond.

Attach lead sheet with quick-
drying bond.

Medium

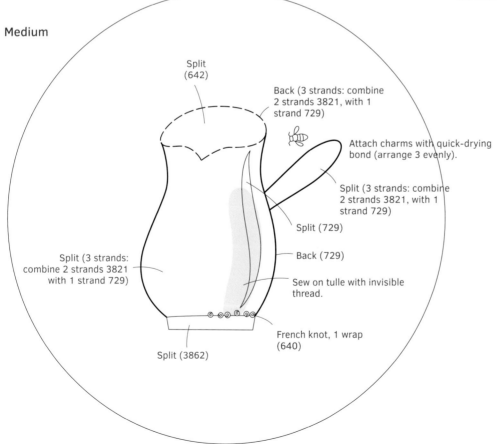

Split
(642)

Back (3 strands: combine
2 strands 3821, with 1
strand 729)

Attach charms with quick-drying
bond (arrange 3 evenly).

Split (3 strands: combine
2 strands 3821, with 1
strand 729)

Split (729)

Back (729)

Sew on tulle with invisible
thread.

Split (3 strands:
combine 2 strands 3821
with 1 strand 729)

French knot, 1 wrap
(640)

Split (3862)

Notes: Apply fusible
interfacing to the reverse
side of the embroidery fabric
before embroidering. Set
the finished work into an
embroidery hoop.

How to Make

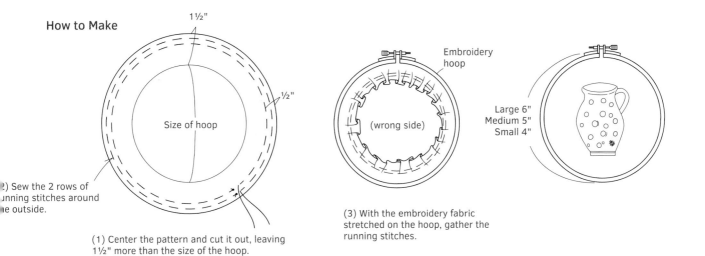

1½"

½"

Size of hoop

(2) Sew the 2 rows of running stitches around the outside.

(1) Center the pattern and cut it out, leaving 1½" more than the size of the hoop.

Embroidery hoop

(wrong side)

Large 6"
Medium 5"
Small 4"

(3) With the embroidery fabric stretched on the hoop, gather the running stitches.

Embroidery Pattern
(actual size)

Use 3 strands, unless noted otherwise.

Large

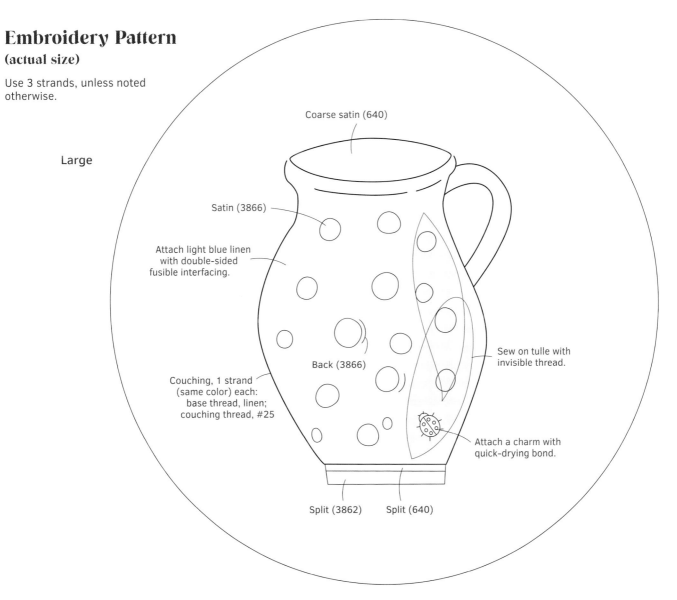

Coarse satin (640)

Satin (3866)

Attach light blue linen with double-sided fusible interfacing.

Back (3866)

Sew on tulle with invisible thread.

Couching, 1 strand (same color) each: base thread, linen; couching thread, #25

Attach a charm with quick-drying bond.

Split (3862)   Split (640)

Flower Vase Pin Cushion (Top)

Thread: DMC embroidery floss
No. 25 (413)

Fabric: Linen, unbleached, 4" x 4"

Other: Large: Fusible interfacing, 4" x 4"; felt, gray, 4" x 4"; polyester filling

Finished size: Refer to the diagram.

Notes: Apply fusible interfacing to the reverse side of the embroidery fabric before embroidering. Follow the instructions to make a pin cushion.

Embroidery Pattern
(actual size)

Use 3 strands, unless noted otherwise.

Use (413) for all stitches.

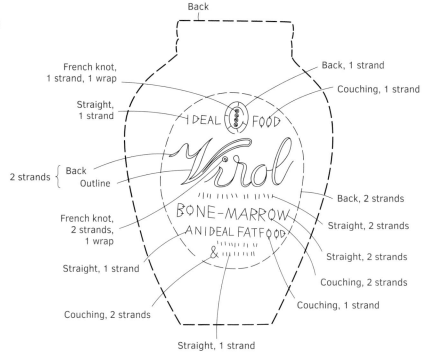

Back

French knot, 1 strand, 1 wrap

Straight, 1 strand

2 strands { Back / Outline

French knot, 2 strands, 1 wrap

Straight, 1 strand

Couching, 2 strands

Straight, 1 strand

Back, 1 strand

Couching, 1 strand

Back, 2 strands

Straight, 2 strands

Straight, 2 strands

Couching, 2 strands

Couching, 1 strand

Pattern for Pin Cushion
Opening (actual size)

Felt, cut 1

How to Make the Pin Cushion

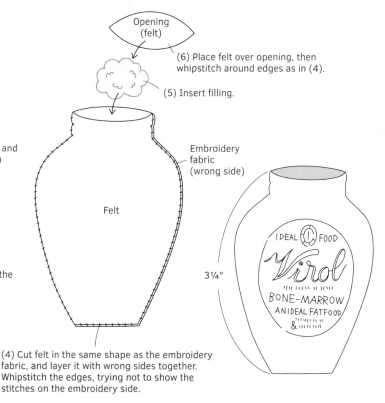

Embroidery fabric

(1) Cut out, leaving a ¼" seam allowance around the outside of the embroidery.

(2) Make cuts at the corners and along the curves of the seam allowance.

(3) Fold the seam allowance toward the wrong side.

Opening (felt)

(6) Place felt over opening, then whipstitch around edges as in (4).

(5) Insert filling.

Felt

Embroidery fabric (wrong side)

3¼"

(4) Cut felt in the same shape as the embroidery fabric, and layer it with wrong sides together. Whipstitch the edges, trying not to show the stitches on the embroidery side.

Flower Vase Pin Cushion (Bottom)

Thread: DMC embroidery floss No. 25 (413)

Fabric: Linen, unbleached, 4" x 4"

Other: Large: Fusible interfacing, 4" x 4"; polyester filling; felt, gray, 8" x 4"; quick-drying bond

Finished size: Refer to the diagram.

Notes: Apply fusible interfacing to the reverse side of the embroidery fabric before embroidering. Follow instructions to make a pin cushion.

Embroidery Pattern
(actual size)

Use 3 strands, unless noted otherwise.

Use (413) for all stitches.

How to Make the Tassel

Linen (front piece)

Finished edge

Cut out, leaving a ¼" seam allowance around the outside (refer to the diagram below).

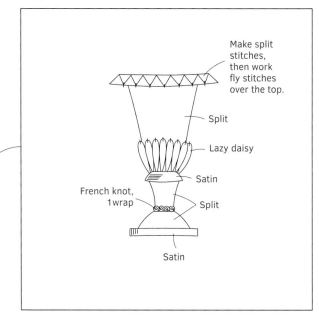

Make split stitches, then work fly stitches over the top.

Split

Lazy daisy

Satin

French knot, 1wrap

Split

Satin

Felt (tassel) Cut 1

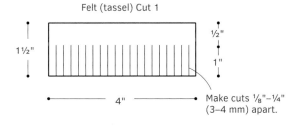

1½"

½"

1"

4"

Make cuts ⅛"–¼" (3–4 mm) apart.

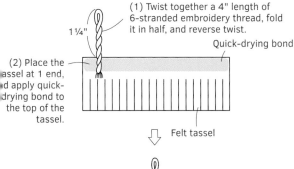

1¼"

(1) Twist together a 4" length of 6-stranded embroidery thread, fold it in half, and reverse twist.

Quick-drying bond

(2) Place the tassel at 1 end, and apply quick-drying bond to the top of the tassel.

Felt tassel

(3) Roll securely from the end with an embroidery twist.

How to Make the Pin Cushion

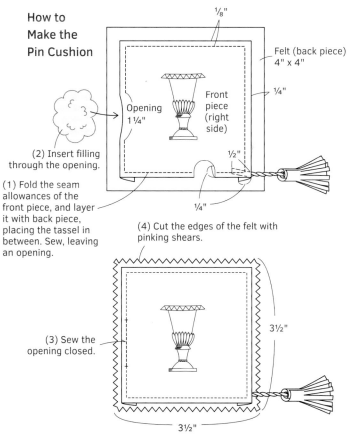

⅛"

Felt (back piece) 4" x 4"

Opening 1¼"

Front piece (right side)

¼"

(2) Insert filling through the opening.

½"

(1) Fold the seam allowances of the front piece, and layer it with back piece, placing the tassel in between. Sew, leaving an opening.

¼"

(4) Cut the edges of the felt with pinking shears.

(3) Sew the opening closed.

3½"

3½"

Afterword

What do you think is the most important thing about embroidering flowers? Color? Shape? Stitching? All of these are important, of course, but if it doesn't "spark joy," then you won't be able to keep your needle going. That feeling that makes my heart tighten—that is inspired by such beauty—is the energy that enables me to choose the colors and create the shapes. That spark is not to be found in the literal color or shape, but it always comes alive in the bouquets created by Yoko Namiki of Gente. I could not have written this book without Yoko's collaboration—over the course of a year, through all four seasons—and without her choosing the fresh flowers that delivered that spark of joy. This book brims with those days spent trying to capture the essence of those bouquets I received. And I'm deeply grateful to Ikue Takizawa and Akiko Suzuki, who accompanied me and took photographs and did styling on that cold day with snow still on the ground when we visited the rose grower; to designer Miho Amano; to Satomi Dairaku, for drawing such easy-to-follow patterns; to my editor who oversaw this lengthy production, Akiko Taniyama; and to all the people who assisted with this book. And finally, I sincerely hope that *Seasonal Flower Embroidery* will deepen your appreciation for embroidery and flowers.

FROM MY ATELIER,
Kazuko Aoki

Kazuko Aoki is an embroidery designer. In her own small garden, she delights in the flowers and plants that she cultivates, as well as the insects and animals that visit, and she incorporates all of these into her embroidery designs. The fabric is her canvas, and her embroidery projects are based on her sketches of garden and field flowers. Known for the unexpected materials she uses in her projects and their abundant originality, her numerous charming projects resonate deeply with many readers and crafters. Aoki's books include *The Embroidered Garden* and *Embroidered Garden Flowers*. Her books have been translated into English, French, Spanish, and Chinese.

Roost Books
An imprint of Shambhala Publications, Inc.
2129 13th Street
Boulder, Colorado 80302
www.roostbooks.com

Originally published as Aoki Kazuko No Hanashishu (NV70529)
Copyright © Kazuko Aoki / Nihon Vogue-sha 2019
English translation rights arranged with Nihon Vogue Corp. through Japan Uni Agency, Inc., Tokyo

Staff credits
Art Direction: Mihoko Amano
Styling: Akiko Suzuki
Photography: Ikue Takizawa, Noriaki Moriya
Floral Designs: Yoko Namiki
Tracing: (day studio) Satomi Dairaku
Editorial Assistance: Rika Tanaka, Motoko Soma, Toshie Yano, Hiroko Suzuki, Keiko Fujimura, Masako Okada
Editor in charge: Akiko Taniyama
Special thanks to Marufuku Herb Farm
(http://marufuku.noen.biz/)
Art Fiber Endo: http://www.artfiberendo.co.jp/

Gente: http://www.gente.jp/

Bibliography: "Floral arrangements inspired by nature," Yoko Namiki Ruteles, Inc.

Roost Designer: Amy Sly

9 8 7 6 5 4 3 2 1

First English Edition
Printed in China

⊗This edition is printed on acid-free paper that meets the American National Standards Institute Z39.48 Standard.
△Shambhala Publications makes every effort to print on recycled paper. For more information please visit www.shambhala.com.
Roost Books is distributed worldwide by Penguin Random House, Inc., and its subsidiaries.

Library of Congress Cataloging-in-Publication Data
Names: Aoki, Kazuko, 1953– author. | Powell, Allison Markin, translator.
Title: Seasonal flower embroidery: a year of stitching wild blooms and botanicals / Kazuko Aoki; translation by Allison Markin Powell.
Other titles: Aoki Kazuko no hana shishu Hanaya gente no hana tayori.
English Description: Boulder: Shambhala, [2022] | Originally published as Aoki Kazuko no hana shishu Hanaya gente no hana tayori by Kazuko Aoki in Japan in 2019 by Nihon Vogue Co., Ltd., Tokyo.
Identifiers: LCCN 2021031488 | ISBN 9781611808926 (paperback)
Subjects: LCSH: Embroidery—Patterns. | Flowers in art. | Decoration and ornament—Plant forms. | Seasons—Miscellanea.
Classification: LCC TT773.A66413 2022 | DDC 746.44—dc23
LC record available at https://lccn.loc.gov/2021031488